CONFESSIONS OF A NAUGHTY MOMMY

HOW I FOUND MY LOST LIBIDO

HEIDI RAYKEIL

SEAL PRESS

CONFESSIONS OF A NAUGHTY MOMMY
How I Found My Lost Libido

Published by
Seal Press
An Imprint of Avalon Publishing Group, Incorporated
1400 65th Street, Suite 250
Emeryville, CA 94608

ISBN-10 1-58005-157-X
ISBN-13 978-1-58005-157-6

9 8 7 6 5 4 3 2

Library of Congress Cataloging-in-Publication Data
Raykeil, Heidi.
Confessions of a naughty mommy : how I found my lost libido / by Heidi Raykeil.
p. cm.
ISBN-13: 978-1-58005-157-6
ISBN-10: 1-58005-157-X
1. Raykeil, Heidi. 2. Mothers—United States—Biography. 3. Wives—United States—Biography. 4. Mothers—Sexual behavior. 5. Sex in marriage. I. Title.
HQ759.R39 2006
306.874'3092—dc22
2005027119

Cover design by Gerilyn Attebery
Interior design by Domini Dragoone
Printed in the United States of America by Worzalla
Distributed by Publishers Group West

For JB

JUA

Contents

FOREPLAY

ZERO-SIX MONTHS

Introduction

Sex in the Suburbs

Here's the thing. You're young, or not so young. You're in love. You're naughty. You have sex madly—wherever, whenever, however you can. You read poems about being each other's missing piece, about completing each other. You *fit.* It's two against the world; you're a pair, a set, partners in crime, two in the hand, the double whammy, *soul mates.* Two sides of the same coin, two sides of the story, 2 hot 2 handle. *Just the two of us.* You are clean, efficient, parallel lines; your passion is direct, unfiltered, raw.

Sex in the Suburbs

And then, literally overnight, two becomes three. "Husband and wife" becomes "mother and father." "Lover" becomes "other"—other roles, other priorities, other loves. Your love life becomes awkward, unbalanced, tipping and toppling: a terribly uneven, unseemly triangle. Bye-bye, parallel lines. Bye-bye, partner in crime. Naughtiness as you know it is over. So long, leisurely mornings in bed; so long, carefree nights carousing; so long, spontaneous summertime sex. Hello, sex in the suburbs.

About five years ago, a hot summer hike turned into hot sweaty sex for my husband, JB, and me: hiked-up shirts and hiked-down shorts and us roughing it in all the right ways. Just off the trail, in the cool shade of a tanoak tree, we risked contracting poison oak in all the wrong places. Hearing other hikers headed our way only added to our heat, and with the snap of a branch, *boom!* Our daughter was conceived.

Although I'm mostly a quiet person, I have always had a naughty side. A fun, risk-taking, whiskey-drinking, dancing-on-the-table side. A do-it-in-the-bushes side. A lap-dance-for-my-husband side. Even as a kid I had it. My imaginary friend, Herina, didn't come to play dolls and have tea parties, she came to wreak havoc, be nasty and crude, loud and mean-spirited. Then Heidi would come back and be sweet and perfect and quiet again.

Naughtiness, to me, is not just about sex—although that's

certainly a big fun part of it. It's about the little imp that sits on my shoulder and tells me to push the limits, bend the rules, take a chance. It's the *Why not?* side of me. It's about fun and excitement, chills and thrills, the feeling of being alive. Of course, that's not exactly compatible with the image of mothering out there: the angel on the other shoulder, sugar and spice, everything nice, *Careful now, careful.*

In her book *The Mother Dance,* Harriet Lerner says, "[M]uch of psychology remains a whodunit with the finger pointed in the mother's direction." She got that right. Ultimately, we're the ones blamed when our kids grow up to be on *Jerry Springer.* We're the ones trying to avoid that by gobbling up parenting books and Baby Einstein videos and baby sign-language classes. Manic mommies everywhere are striving for perfection, in their kids, in themselves. We're striving to hold it all together, to figure out working and not working, to choose the best schools, the best parenting styles, the best future for the people who mean more to us than anything.

Naughtiness, to me, *is not just about sex—although that's certainly a big fun part of it.*

It's a crazy, beautiful madness that takes its toll, wears us out, and doesn't allow a whole heck of a lot of room to be naughty. Beyond that, with the baby-ization of Hollywood—Gwyneth Paltrow and Kate Hudson and the beautiful Desperate Housewives on Wisteria Lane—we're supposed to look like a million bucks, too. But we don't have personal trainers; we have potty training. We don't have our own Nanny 911 or personal chefs; we have Chef Boyardee, and we have our hot local firefighters showing up while we're in the bathroom because our toddler dialed 911 by accident, *again.* The glossy magazines we zone out on while we're in that bathroom, hiding out, promise to help us have it all, do it all: You *can* be the perfect mom and the perfect wife, they assure us. You can be holy, happy, housewifey, *and* a whore in the bedroom. But four and a half years ago, that sure wasn't my reality.

Four and a half years ago, my sex life tanked because I gave birth to the most beautiful, precious, gentle little person I have ever met, my daughter Ramona. And then I sat dumbstruck and watched as she completely obliterated my love life. Where once my husband and I had stayed up until 3 AM bouncing each other off the walls, now we were up at 3 taking turns bouncing her on our knees, desperate to get her back to bed.

Despite getting an extensive sex education, starting with my parents and ending with a lot of personal mistakes,

I was totally unprepared for the toll motherhood would take on my marriage. This isn't to say I didn't receive plenty of information: From the minute my swollen belly announced my pregnancy to the world, people gave me advice about parenting. They told me (whether I asked or not) their thoughts on crib vs. co-sleeping, breast vs. bottle, diaper service vs. disposables. They told me I'd be tired, more tired than I've ever been before. They told me I'd never regret it, that it's hard, that there's nothing better.

But no one ever told me I would end up calling my husband "Poppy" when I used to call him "lover." Or that soon I'd find sleeping to be the most satisfying part of sleeping with him. No seasoned mom ever slipped a bottle of Probe or Liquid Silk into my baby shower basket with a little note letting me know that nursing can cause vaginal dryness. No one explained to me not to do it in front of mirrors that first year, or to avoid walking by stacks of dirty dishes on the way to the bedroom, or not to waste any time and just say up front, "If you touch my boobs, all bets are off."

Just say up front, "If you touch my boobs, **ALL BETS ARE OFF."**

And no one warned me that having a baby was like the excitement of falling in love all over again, except with someone much younger and better smelling than my husband. No one told me that for all intents and purposes, having a baby was dangerously similar to having an affair.

In 2002, Oprah aired one of her most talked-about segments: "What Your Mother Never Told You About Motherhood." I remember the excitement and tears the following day in the new moms' group I had recently joined. Finally someone had discussed—on national television—what we had been whispering about every week. The truth about motherhood was out of the closet for us new moms: It's not all joy and onesies and warmth. Breastfeeding can be a bitch, sleep deprivation sucks, and even the best relationships take a hit when the baby shows up. It's not always easy; it's not always natural. We can't all be Carol Brady or Claire Huxtable, and we can't all get off on scrapbooking and scraped knees. I watched as the books given at baby showers changed from the sunny, if rigid, *What to Expect When You're Expecting* to the grittier *Operating Instructions: A Journal of My Son's First Year* and *Breeder: Real-Life Stories from the New Generation of Mothers.* Motherhood was getting a much-needed makeover, an in-your-face, warts-and-all truth-telling; the stodgy old role was being revamped and reclaimed as cool and hip.

And yet—as I made my way through this new motherhood, there was one subject us savvy and swinging New Mothers still rarely heard much about (occasional *Oprah* episode aside). Sex. After. Baby. And our lack of it. The sad truth is that many of us do-it-all moms of today seem to be doing everything except, well, *it*. One recent study shows that married couples today have less sex than they had in the sexually repressed '50s. Even Dr. Phil has called sexless marriages "an epidemic." But most of the parents I know don't need Dr. Phil to tell us we're sex-starved. We whisper it to each other when the kids are asleep; we hear murmurs of it over too many glasses of wine, at mothers' groups and playgrounds and girls' nights out.

Let me confess. I started this journey for strictly selfish reasons: I wanted to be naughty again! One day I woke up out of the fog of new motherhood and discovered that somewhere along the line, I had lost my libido. Although I didn't miss sex, I did miss wanting sex. I missed the old naughty parts of my life; I missed my husband. What happened to those wild days and nights when we couldn't keep our hands off each other? What happened to *us?* Though I could of course answer this in part, I also felt like I was the only one in the world not having mind-blowing sex every day of the week. Or even not-so-great sex once every couple of weeks. It wasn't until I mentioned this in my mothers' group one day that I realized I was far from the only one. The other mothers were desperate to hear others' stories and share details of their disintegrating sex lives. I soon learned my sex life wasn't the worst, but it certainly wasn't the best either. Their details were always vague, but the emotions were the same: bitterness, confusion, and a sad but uninspired longing for *the way things were.* They echoed my own feelings.

What happened to those wild days and nights when we **COULDN'T KEEP OUR HANDS OFF EACH OTHER?**

I wanted sexiness to be a part of my life again—not like lose ten pounds sexy, or wear rashy underwear sexy, or put on makeup I'll rub off at naptime sexy. I wanted to think sexy. Write sexy. Maybe even *have sexy.* With new determination, I decided to fight the good fight and take on my lost libido, to hunt it down like I would chocolate after midnight.

I decided to become a private detective: Trixie Belden or Nancy Drew or a Bobbsey twin (only older and hotter and quite a bit naughtier). I'd become the Thin Man, the bumbling private detective of libido hunting—only I'm a woman and not as thin as I'd like to be, and I drink red wine instead of martinis. But still, I was on the case, hot on the trail.

I read books like *Hot Monogamy: Essential Steps to More Passionate, Intimate Lovemaking* (even though I could never manage to stay up past 8 PM to follow through on the prescribed exercises). I read magazines with one-size-fits-all sex cures and articles that offered Six Easy Steps That Will Have You Saying *Yes* to Sex, and Ten Ways to End Charity Sex. I tried their suggestions. I tried to nap when the baby naps. I scheduled "date night," bought our daughter a "big girl" bed, and even started shaving my legs.

As I made my way back to my sexual self, I found myself exploring relationships with the usual libido-sucking suspects: sheer exhaustion, that love affair with the baby, the shrill hormones (oxytocin, prolactin, thyroid, testosterone) whose fluctuations played havoc with my system. I tried to look at life as my husband does, through a lens of lust-colored glasses, and considered why he hadn't had the same problems transitioning his unflagging sex drive into parenthood. I snooped around such seedy undesirables as body changes, hemorrhoid-induced 'rhoid rage, deep-seated spousal resentment, childhood hang-ups, and the terror of being forever trapped in a minivan. Hot on the case, I bumbled my way through a series of experiments, treading close to matrimonial danger as my desire for the naughty ol' life I had Before Baby kicked into high gear.

I also started documenting this hunt by writing a column

called "Sex in the Suburbs" for the online magazine *Literary Mama* in 2003, using the byline "the Naughty Mommy." *What does your husband think?* people asked after reading details about our fights, our making up, our open book of a sex life (or lack thereof). *What about your parents?* But my parents and my husband know me; they know I'm an emotional incontinent. They know I can't hold what I'm feeling in—I just plop it all out there. That's what I do with my girlfriends; it's why I love reality TV; it's why, yes, I love *Oprah*! Besides that, honesty about sex runs in my family: My dad is an HIV/AIDS health educator, and my mom has written an erotic film (an excerpt from her latest email: "My daughter is writing like such a slut . . . I'm so proud!"). As for my husband, he was getting more sex out of the deal than ever (how could I be a sex columnist and never have sex?), which made sharing the intimate details of our lives with strangers plenty worth it to him.

How could I be a sex columnist and **NEVER HAVE SEX?**

Originally I hoped that by sharing my own confessions on the sad state of my sex life, I would get moms, including myself, thinking more deeply about sex—and at the very least, I thought I was writing a lighthearted humor column that might give others a good laugh at my expense. But once I started writing, I was blown away by the letters I got from mothers. Most of them weren't lighthearted; they weren't laughing or sexy or tongue-in-cheek back at me. Some were desperate, some were excited, and almost every one said thank you—thank you for saying what I'm feeling, thank you for making me feel I'm not so alone. "*Thanks for helping us feel our wholeness—naughty, confused, compassionate, sweet, paranoid, imperfect, loved, empowered . . .* " "*Thank you for doing what you do . . . it makes a HUGE difference to me. There are things you talk about that I fear to say . . . and when you do I feel better.*" "*Thanks for helping me to remember that I want to wake up from this. . . . You've made me feel like I'm not alone, and that I have it in me to get past this.*"

So much for lighthearted and funny. The thing is, Sex After Baby is taboo for a reason—it's not a light, breezy topic. It's huge and highly charged, it's complicated, it's deep and mind-boggling at times. And none of the magazines and cheesy six-step exercises can, in themselves, teach you how to find your way back to good sex, because rediscovering real sexual connection is a process. It's messy and beautiful and evolving, like us. Sex is hard enough. Marriage is hard enough. But take away sleep and add overwhelming love for this other little person, and watch out! There's a reason they haven't discovered a Viagra for women yet—our libidos are so complicated the prescription would have to come with bells and whistles and coupons for things like housecleaning and therapy. (Or better yet, it would come with a home lobotomy kit, complete with instructions for turning off our "mother" roles and turning on instant feelings of intimacy.)

Ultimately, I found, it wasn't greeting my husband at the door in Saran Wrap, using mint-flavored condoms, or planning a weekend away that helped us revamp our romance. It wasn't advice books, clothes, or a new haircut that made me feel sexy again. It wasn't doing my Kegels or trying the striptease-aerobics class at my gym that got things rolling. What always got me going again was simply that old fashioned kick-starter: connection. It was the sense that I wasn't alone in this. It was laughing with other moms at the park about which Wiggle is the sexiest (the Wiggles being an Australian musical group hugely popular with the preschool set—and it's definitely Anthony, you can tell he's a bad boy when he's not being all . . . Wiggly). It was hugging a new mom as she cried in relief because she knew someone's sex life was even worse than hers. It was emailing someone who felt she was going through exactly the same thing I was. It was talking for hours—to my mom, my friends, my sister-in-law, my therapist, and, of course, my dear husband—about how complicated sex is, how I like it and don't like it, how hard it is to balance, how I love him, how he drives me crazy, how we blink and everything changes. It was this dialogue, this confessing and truth telling, that reconnected me to a passionate life—to other grown-up human beings, to my husband, and, most importantly, to myself.

This book is divided into four parts; each one represents a certain time in my daughter's growth, and in my growth as a mother and a partner. Each of these sections is written from the mental space I was in at that time. During many of those times, I couldn't exactly see the path I was on; I couldn't see my husband, or myself, in quite the same light we shine in most days now. As I wrote, my editor kept saying, "More sex!" and "Keep it light!" I tried, I really did, to keep things light and sexy and funny, but I kept coming back to the truth about Sex After Baby: Some of it is fun. Some of it is light. But a lot of it's not. The truth is, marriage is hard. Parenting is hard. Sex is hard. Heck, happiness is hard. My husband and I are in a sexual upswing right now, and we're closer than ever, but I know that, like my own libido, this situation's not static. Like any good mystery, we will have our ups and downs, our turns and twists and one-armed bad guys to contend with. I know our closeness will come and go, it will be all over the map—one minute overpowering us and then suddenly, shockingly gone, leaving only a trail, a shadow, a glass slipper.

The story of finding my lost libido is no fairytale—it's not all Prince Charming and happy endings. Plenty of days I'm still more "mommy" than "naughty." When I'm stressed or I've had a bad day, the first thing to go is my libido. Just a couple nights ago, under the stress of trying to finish this book, I found my husband waiting up for me in bed. When I climbed in with him, he put his arm around me and I snapped, "There's *no way* we're having sex tonight!" Really he was just trying to connect with me, to actually just put his arm around me, but that's how it goes. Four years ago, that would have launched a weeklong fight. It would have hurt feelings and hit buttons. But now, it didn't. We went to sleep, talked about it in the morning, and made jokes about it, and by the afternoon, after writing a particularly potent sex scene for the book, I ended up naked on the black leather couch in his office. He ended up getting his connection, and I ended up liking it, a lot.

Here are a few other things no one really tells you about Sex After Baby: No one tells you how good it can be. No one tells you that fighting to find that lost libido is definitely worth it. No one mentions that something about the combination of childbirth and hormones and the deep bond of parenthood can make sex so much more satisfying. Or how waiting

How fun and naughty *sneaking off during naptime can be.*

and waiting and wanting can make it that much sweeter. Or how fun and naughty sneaking off during naptime can be. No one says, "Three words, honey: *quality, not quantity.*"

I may have started looking to solve this mystery for selfish purposes—which, amazingly enough, seems to have worked—but somewhere along the line, I began to hope for something bigger. I'm not exactly thrilled at the prospect of having people I know and care about reading the most private details of my sex life—my in-laws, my friends' parents, my dad, my daughter's teacher. But somehow, during this whole process, a little potential awkwardness at family reunions or preschool pickup began seeming like a small price to pay for someone, somewhere, to feel a little less alone in the world. Though this book is about sex, it's also about being true to yourself and holding on to your identity even when you're connected so closely to someone else. My parents taught me, growing up, to above all else tell the truth and help others. And that's what I'm trying to do. I want mothers out there to keep telling the truth—to each other, to our partners, to society—about what we're really like and what we really need. I want us to feel safe letting out our inner naughties, and to have fun doing it. I want us to become "thinkaboutsexaholics"—or to at least *occasionally* think about sex. I want us to let ourselves feel hot again, and let ourselves off the hook when we don't. I want to give this confused virgin-mother society a little push in the direction of sexy. And I want to let all those other sexy, tired, uptight, dry, stretched, sewn, poked, pulled, milked, saggy, hot, hairy, awesomely unstoppable mamas out there know they're not alone.

TICKET TO THE MOON

CHAPTER 1

We're gonna have the same phone number
for a long time
we're gonna have all our friends come over
for the football game
for barbeques
go shopping for shoes
each day will be pretty much the same
boooring boooring
same shit year after year
but I'm happy enough just having you here

—"THE BORING SONG" BY JB BERNASKI

there's something about the word "wife" that just doesn't inspire naughtiness. It conjures up images of station wagons and oversized, flesh-colored undergarments. And when "wife" becomes "mother," forgettaboutit. In the realm of domesticity, hotness seems to disappear. Married life becomes a one-way ticket to Dullsville.

Don't get me wrong. I love not worrying about STDs, or heartbreak, or heartbreaking. I love having my best friend there to share the thrill of growing a person, to catch me, to push me, to inspire me, to support me. I love spending Saturday afternoons together at Waterbabies and Saturday nights at the video store, I really do. I even love the lazy familiarity of married sex, on those rare occasions when opportunity and libido converge on quiet Sunday afternoons.

But as much as I love this domestic bliss, it's about as hot as dirty underwear. And it's certainly not the naughtiness we started with: the fast, furious alley fucks, the bar-bathroom quickies, the motel mania. We started young and on fire in San Francisco, in a one-night stand that had other ideas, that soon took on a life of its own, and became the rightness that today is us. In late summer of 1993, when I was twenty-one, I met a guy—JB—in my local bar and took him home with me. Four years after that, he asked me to marry him, in the backseat of an old Cadillac. Classy? Not really. Naughty? Just enough.

We celebrated our engagement by taking off to Las Vegas with another couple we were friends with. They were older (they must have been in their *thirties* or something) and married, but they didn't act either. They nearly out-partied us and quite possibly out-naughtied us, calling us from the room next door to make sure we were getting the same cable porn station as them, then making sure we heard them making the most of it through the paper-thin walls. By the end of the night we were all at Club Paradise, sharing a table and beers and a lovely stripper. *That's how we'll be,* I thought, watching the other couple, worked up by the way they looked at each other, inflamed by the way I caught my future husband looking at me; absolutely, positively, sure.

I rarely see that look anymore. What I see now are looks of expectation, of familiarity, of comfortable scrutiny. I see him differently now, too. Instead of a partner, I sometimes see him more as a giant, oversized toddler than a man; waddling with want, incapable of completing the smallest task without direction, and always hungry with need. I'm sure he sees me differently, too. I often feel more like a wild mother bear than a partner—I'm fierce, I'm unpredictable, I'm hairy.

Back when we met, we were electric, dynamic, frenetic. We spent hours in bed exchanging secrets and dreams we never believed would come true: that we'd go camping once we had cars; that somehow we'd figure out how to grow up and be real people together; that we'd have two kids and name them Johnny and Ramona. Back then we wrote each other love letters in bad Italian and took dirty Polaroids of ourselves wearing too few clothes. We were desperate—for connection, for hope, for each other.

These days we are comfortable. Now, instead of love notes, we write Post-it notes. "Yard this weekend!" "Take out garbage!" "Diapers!" Now, instead of taking dirty Polaroids, we pick up vast stacks of photos from Costco, all centered around the same angelic subject, the two of us barely noticeable in the periphery, hanging around like bloated and very tired-looking ghosts. We're still desperate: to find our way back to that connection, that excitement, that spark we had when we first got together—or at least some semblance of it.

I think back to the night we met. "You probably have a girlfriend or something," I said, staring at the ceiling of my Haight Street flat in San Francisco. I couldn't bring myself to look at the stranger lying next to me, the man I had no way of knowing would one day become my husband. Never mind that we had just slapped skin, swapped sweat, hit all four corners of my room like a gymnastics competition. Suddenly I was shy, insecure, sick with twinges of

Never mind that we had just hit all four corners of my room like a **GYMNASTICS COMPETITION**

regret. In other words, way too sober. Not like the night before, when we'd danced on the bar together, stumbled home to my flat, and shared my bed.

He turned and stared at me, inches from my face. I blushed and turned to the side, embarrassed at his ease and freaked out by his intensity, his controlled confidence in that raw moment. He ran a finger over my naked back, like he was spelling something out. At the base of my spine, he stopped, then spread a warm hand over my hip and tugged me closer to him. I turned back over as he rested his hand on my knee.

"I have someone I see."

He was nonchalant, the way he said it, a side thought. But I caught sadness in his face as he joined me in staring at the ceiling again.

That's how we started—naughty by nature. A wild, grab-life-by-the-horny-boy night that somehow turned into "till death do us part." What my future husband didn't tell me at the time was that he had someone he "saw" every day when he woke up—a live-in girlfriend he was in an "open relationship" with (so very San Francisco). That they shared a happy, normal life he'd worked very hard to get: playing house and going to school, hosting dinner parties and political meetings. He also didn't tell me he was simmering inside. He didn't tell me that despite his golden-boy looks, his tawny confidence, he was shattered and black inside from a childhood of pain and just waiting to blow the whole act up. And he didn't tell me that I was just the girl to help him do it.

Of course, there were things I didn't tell him that night, either. I didn't tell him about the other guys I was sleeping with: the bookstore guy, the white guy with dreads, the artist. I didn't tell him that no matter how many guys I ended up with, I left feeling emptier, lower, more hungover each time. I didn't tell him about the anxiety that had taken ahold of me, how my mind latched obsessively onto hard pieces of worry, polishing them into shiny bits, compulsively going over them again and again, and holding on to them desperately like a child holding a prized piece of weathered sea glass. I didn't tell him how I self-medicated with alcohol and men and anything else that made me feel good, however short-lived.

The truth is, I was never a slut for the sake of sex. Really I was a slut for love—an intimacy junkie. And sex was just how I got my fix. I lived for pillow talk, for the in-between moments of connection where physical proximity and emotional confession converged. I thrived off the seeds of self-disclosure men would share in those moments, the temporary thrill of knowing another person so intimately, the way I felt so close and needed and chosen. In those moments, I mattered. In those moments, I could show the desperation and need I usually kept hidden.

I disguised those feelings as want and lust, and used them to slip into men's weak spots and chinks in their armor, leaving them open and vulnerable. My territory now, my chance to fill my needy bowl, to lap up closeness and connection and to rest, sated, smoking cigarettes with them in the quiet afterglow.

This is who we were then: young, empty, desperate, and off track, but crazy in love and willingly stumbling toward each other and a life we weren't yet sure of.

Fast-forward seven years. "I think something has come between us," my husband whispers to me across the bed, and we laugh together as he points to our three-month-old baby daughter, sprawled out horizontally between us.

In some ways, the first several months of parenting have brought us closer together than ever before. We laugh together at Ramona's funny face; she's our funny valentine, born two days before Valentine's Day. She is a weak-chinned, floppy-armed, solemn little raisin, perfect and familiar in every way. She is sunshine, light, warmth. She lies on my chest and heat burns through me with a ferocity that feels like heartbreak, only hopeful and happy, but just as sharp. My husband spoons us both from the side, our nascent triangle a perfect fit. He sings to us, his voice husky with exhaustion and emotion. "*You make me smile in my heart . . .* "

Everything is about her: *What does the baby need, Can*

we bring the baby, Oh, look at the baby. We have completely cocooned. We rarely see friends, we rarely go out; we do everything as a unit. It would be easy to blame it on exhaustion, and in part, we do. But it's more than that: It's baby bliss, it's the wonderfully womblike quality of this quiet new life. It's the fourth trimester and we are also newborn, blinking at the outside world, dazed and dreamy and hungry for the familiar, for the immediate. In many ways, this is the life neither one of us grew up with but both of us wanted. It's safe, nuclear, quiet, and comfortable. It's sweatpant life.

But as close and comfortable as we are, I feel something shifting. My husband is no longer the center of my world, my number one, my go-to guy. Some *thing* has come between us: a thing that stirs my heart in the way he used to when we first met. A beautiful baby whose reciprocating smile floods me with tipsy satisfaction and a kind of quiet that makes nothing else seem to matter.

Let me confess. The night I met my future husband, it was not love at first sight. Nothing nearly that romantic. That's not to say I didn't notice him checking me out, or that I didn't think he was cute, with his shaved head and friendly eyes. I did, but at the time I was actually hoping to run into someone else, another guy I was attempting a fumbling relationship with based on our youthful mutual interest in drinking and making out.

At one point I even left the bar and stumbled up the street to bang on the door of his flat. But I got lucky. My makeout buddy never showed, and I ended up back at the bar, where the man who would become my husband charmed me (his real line—no joke—"I'd buy you a drink, but I hear the age of chivalry is over"), lost to me in pool (best of five), and eventually walked me home (for "safety reasons," he still claims).

That night, I knew he was different from the usual men I ended up with. Maybe it was the way he wouldn't have sex with me until I'd drank the pot of coffee he made and sobered up, or the fact that he used a condom without any discussion or awkwardness. Maybe it was the way my ever-pessimistic and overly protective roommate drunkenly wrapped his arm around my shoulder and said, "I *like* this guy." Or maybe it was simply the fact that he was wearing pajama bottoms as pants, in public. Whatever it was though, I noticed it. And while we didn't end up away from each other for very long, in the morning he was gone and I was left, again, empty and wistful.

All these years later, I still don't know exactly why the two of us are so good together. Although neither one of us turned out to be exactly whom the other expected (I thought he was a super-together guy; he thought I was a walking wrecking ball), somehow we're still perfect for each other. I still love his unfailing self-confidence—to this day it blows me away. (Case in point: He's only recently noticed the extra pounds he's put on. No matter what the reality is when he looks into a mirror, he sees Adonis shining back.) And somehow, maybe because of that confidence, he has never been put off or threatened by my neurotic insecurities and oversensitivity. Somehow, it gives him life, it makes him feel at home with me and open to the world in a way he couldn't be without me.

My husband believes we have a love of the ages. He thinks we were meant to be—we're fated, we're one of "those" couples. Two months after we met, he moved out of the apartment he lived in with his girlfriend and told me he needed a month to figure out the right thing to do. I was terrified that in that month he would change his mind, go back home to her, and never come back. I didn't beg him to stay, but I wanted to. I wanted to throw myself at his feet, wrap my arms around his leg, and keep him from going anywhere but inside my room, my bed, me. Instead I played it cool, telling him to do what he had to do. I might wait for him, I might not. But that night, in bed, as we said our goodbyes, and then said them again and again as thoroughly as we could, he touched my face and told me to remember this day, remember the date. Later he told me that was the day he knew we were right together, the day he knew choosing me would be the best thing he would ever do.

Looking back, I have to agree with him: It's hard for me to

say our relationship was anything but fate. There are all sorts of different ways we could have met, so many places our lives had in common: We both went to San Francisco State University, we had friends with less than six degrees of separation, we went to see author Alex Haley read at the same community college event. By coincidence, we even both worked at the same child-care center in Seattle. We never met, but I got the position that opened up when he left, so we knew the same children.

My husband still laughs when I press him about why he gambled everything on me that first night, and why he stayed with me well after he knew I was a lot more complicated than the pool-playing, whiskey-drinking girl he met in the bar that night.

"I was broken," he says, working the pensive emotion he knows I can't resist. "I was broken and you were so damn hot!"

Amen to that.

We were hot. We were young and beautiful and desperate in a sweltering San Francisco Indian summer. Once we worked out the initial kinks (that girlfriend, those damn pajama pants), we were unstoppable. Our separate needs battled for satiety, resulting in endless attraction and intensity. We were consumed and passionate. We forgot to eat. We skipped classes to stare at each other, we went to parties and danced only with each other, and we went to rock shows and sweated only on each other. And whew, were we naughty!

If sex is a form of communication, we were on the unlimited calling plan. We communicated in the park, in dark corners, in barroom bathrooms. We stayed in bed for days, getting up only to go drinking or to the occasional job or class. We communicated our way into our first apartment together, communicated the night after he met my mom for the first time, communicated on the side of the road on the way up to Reno to visit his brother in prison.

If sex is a form of communication, we were on the UNLIMITED CALLING PLAN.

We had, in fact, just finished communicating in the backseat of his dad's old Cadillac when he popped the question four and a half years after that fateful first night.

"Why don't you be my wife?"

Just like that. He knew it was what I wanted, what I'd been pushing for the past couple years. Like everything between us, his proposal was heated and impulsive. There was no ring or elaborate scheme, no chilled champagne or family members hiding around the corner. There was just us, caught up in a moment and each other and the sound of rain on the roof and cheesy pop music on the radio. This is how we were then: uncensored, immediate, volatile. There were no inhibitions, nothing between us but air. The depth and directness of our bond filled us both up, made us feel safe and complete. Lying in bed, we were always amazed at the way our bodies fit, at the wholeness two slightly broken people could make.

With everyone else in my life I've always used a filter; I think before I speak, I shut down, I fake it. I've pretended to be happy when I wasn't, pretended I didn't care when I did, pretended things were fine when they weren't. With my husband, everything hangs out. Our love is free-flowing, unfiltered. Over the years we discovered ourselves together: the real me, the real him. We cleaned each other up, straightened each other out, forgave each other, let each other in. I gave myself to him wholly and completely, and he did the same. On our wedding day, in front of seventy-five family members and friends, he couldn't stop crying long enough to say his vows. Each time he got to the "with all that I am, and all that I have" part, he broke down, sputtering and floored that I would have him so completely, that we would be there for each other no matter what.

Domesticity had always been mythical to us. Years before we tied the knot we'd lie around in bed going over hypothetical names for hypothetical babies, testing each one's nickname potential and schoolyard vulnerability. I'd climb naked on top of JB and bring him just to the edge, moving slowly over him, daring him. "Let's make a baby, Baby," I'd say, trying to lure him into a life-altering mistake. "You know you want to. . . . " But he would just smile. Despite our rock-and-roll lifestyle he was always responsible, always clearheaded when it came to birth control. On stage with his geek-punk-pop band he'd answer me, thrashing and sweating and screaming and singing ("like Neil Young on methamphetamines," according to one reviewer) about babymaking and life growing up with his teenage mom: *I'm only twenty-two already thinkin' bout cul de sacs/she's only twenty-one already thinkin' bout lying on her back/in a hospital sack/with the nurse screaming push push push./Too young to be a daddy but too old to be a kid/so I just might end up doing just what my daddy did/ have one young/might be fun/then again what's the rush rush rush?*

My husband's childhood makes mine look like a day with the Cleavers. His mother was fourteen when she had him. With no biological father in the picture, the two of them did the best they could on their own, on San Francisco's seventies-era fringes. Even after he was adopted by his mom's new husband, his life was chaotic. He fought tooth and nail to pull himself and his younger brother out of their unhappy existence and live healthy everyday lives. His efforts almost worked; he starred in high school plays and shined in college, until his brother started using drugs and made one mistake too many because of them, ending up, at just eighteen, with a seven-year sentence in a state prison.

While I would never call my own childhood traumatic, it was certainly confusing. I grew up in Seattle, in a huge hippie house filled with people coming and going: young Jesuit volunteers, homeless families, immigrants, my destitute alcoholic grandfather. It was never quiet; there was always a guitar playing, a rallying speech, a heated community meeting. It smelled like rotten food; boxes of bruised fruit and past-pull-date dairy sat in the storeroom, waiting to be revamped as healthy dinners and sent to the soup kitchen my parents founded in a church down the street.

As a young child I dreamed of a quiet, predictable nuclear family and spent hours playing "normal house"—rocking and feeding and sewing up tattered dolls and stuffed animals with worn-thin fur. "*My own home,*" I'd sing along with the dark-haired little girl on the *Jungle Book* record I'd play over and over again as she sang of handsome husbands and children of her own.

By the time I met my own handsome husband-to-be, I was living a kind of double life. At night I'd whoop it up, being naughty and carefree, fun lovin' and careless. We'd go to shows together, move and jump and sweat, his arms wrapped around me, his bony hips and warm spot pushing into me from behind. Hanging out with our friends and old-timers at dive bars, we'd shoot pool, drink loaded gin and tonics, and pick up strangers to bring home for all-night hootanannies. Then JB and I would sneak off to my room and welcome the morning with a bang, falling asleep in each other's arms until the alarm clock went off and I started my daytime life—my responsible, on-track life, going to school and working at the campus childcare center.

Caregiving was an easy profession for me to slip into. I'd watched my parents give and give as social activists, and I was a natural-born nurturer. It was my dream; it was what I'd practiced for so many years, pinning diapers on ragged dolls and babysitting the hippie kids who ran naked through our house. I was good at it, too. I loved the energy of the preschool room, the politics of four-year-olds. I squatted with toddlers, sharing their wonder at a pigeon or guiding their chubby hands as they fumbled with independence. But it was the infant-room shifts that stole my heart: the quietly shared trust, the toothless grins. I was especially good at getting tired babies to sleep. I'd swaddle them up like tiny sausages, then gently rock back and forth in the pastel glider. *Hush-a-bye, don't you cry; go to sleep my little baby.* I'd watch as they struggled to keep their eyes open, then *boom*—just like that, they were out, and I'd touch their little hands and still mouths, imagining my own baby before laying them neatly in their cribs and marking the time on the info sheet I'd later hand their proud parents.

I'd get my fantasy-family fix at work, then head out to the

dive-bar world at the other end of the spectrum, with its unseemly pickup politics, stumbling grownups, and toothless alcoholics. I'd meet JB for drinks and then off we'd go into the night, into bed, my seamless transition from Land of Nod to Land of Naughty.

Back then, domestic salvation was our dream, our pie in the sky, the new romance. We both wanted kids; we both thought in some way it would make the broken parts of ourselves right.

But domestic reality has proven a little bit different. While *making* a baby was so much fun to do together, *having* a baby together . . . mmm . . . not always so much fun. The bond itself is brilliant, golden, unbreakable. But it takes a little getting used to. Things get lost in the meantime, mired in the stew of exhaustion and mother-fog. Connections are missed, feelings are hurt, hormones are unrelenting and volatile.

In the first few months after our daughter's birth we were in the springtime of our lives. We had the happy domesticity we both always wanted; we were a family. A *family.* We were three, the magic number: Bears, Stooges, Wise Men. JB and I should've been fucking like bunnies, getting fat on all that love. But something was wrong. Something was missing. And for the first time in our life together, there were things I wasn't telling JB—and things he wasn't telling me.

Ticket to the Moon

At my six-week postpartum checkup, my OB gave me the green light to, as she so romantically put it, "resume sexual relations" as soon as I felt ready. *Ready? Hmm,* I thought, *there must be some way I can bribe her.* I wanted a signed note like the ones I used to forge to get out of PE class, I wanted a get-out-of-jail-free card, I wanted to buy a little more off-limits time before I had to even think about being ready for sex, before I had to think about getting things back to normal.

Back to normal. I didn't even know what *normal* was anymore. Even before we got married, when it came to sex, *normal* had started to change. After being together for five years, we had already mostly demoted sex to weekends or days off. We were already getting lazy and comfortable living together, taking our relationship for granted, zoning out on TV together and fighting over whose turn it was to take the dog out or how to discipline her when she ate our shoes, or the guitar, or the couch, *again.*

Normal was even more confusing after my daughter's birth. Was it normal to be more turned on by your bed than your husband? Was it normal to be strangely aroused and satisfied by nursing? To want to make out with your three-month-old baby just because you love her so damn much?

Before the baby, the longest time we had gone without sex was three weeks, when JB was in Italy with his grandmother. I'll never forget the reunion sex we had the night he got back.

We weren't living together yet and we both had roommates, so we met in a bar near Polk Street. I dressed more sluttishly than usual, but didn't get many looks for it in the mostly gay neighborhood. We were nervous and jumpy, making dumb small talk and asking questions we'd already answered a million times over the phone. Halfway through our second round of drinks I complimented him on his shirt, then sat across from him with my legs spread enough that he could see I'd purposefully forgotten my panties. Unable to stand it anymore, he slammed some bills on the table and grabbed my arm, and we made a beeline for the hotel room he'd reserved. We stayed up all night in that room, making up for lost time. Clothes were torn, buttons were popped, bodies were bitten, as I showed him how much I missed him, then I showed him again, and again. Then he wooed me with talk of taking me to Italy and showing me off as his wife. It was the first time he'd brought up the "W" word, and I ate it up. By morning, we both could hardly walk. I was as hungover and raw and sore and flutter-hearted as if it had been our first time.

Since then, reunion sex had always been sweet for us, charged and intense like make-up sex after a fight; if we were apart for even a weekend we would make up for it, before and after the fact.

Not exactly how I would describe our post-baby coitus, two months after I gave birth. Despite my fear (it had been a long time) and my total and complete lack of desire, making love for the first time after the baby was born was surprisingly sweet. I knew my husband was ready. I could feel him stare hungrily at me as I walked around the house shirtless. I felt him rise when our feet accidentally grazed in bed, our bodies shifting to accommodate a late-night feeding. As we began to move against each other I wasn't turned on, but I was open to the chance that maybe once we started I'd get caught up in it, forget the baby was asleep in the room with us, and magically switch gears into lover mode. I didn't, but despite the discomfort it felt vaguely nice, familiar and gentle. "Do you want to stop?" My husband would ask, his voice full of desire and concern as we fumbled and *ouch*ed and *okay*ed. "You can change your mind," he said more than once, getting closer. This is my husband at his best: sensitive, sweet, thoughtful, and seconds away from satisfaction.

Like make-up sex after a fight, our reunion sex is always CHARGED AND INTENSE.

One of the first baby items we bought after finding out I was pregnant was a super-expensive, high-quality baby monitor. I'd fantasized about drinking wine and making love by the fireplace, our baby sleeping peacefully in another room, the monitor quiet and assuring on the mantle. But reality is so much different. The baby slept on my chest; she was always within sight, within earshot. Not because we didn't have a room to put her in and close the door (hers was actually the nicest room in the house) or because we didn't have a good enough monitor (it had a mile radius, come on!), but because we were so dumbstruck, so totally in love with this chaos-inducing diaper-bomb that we couldn't imagine doing things any other way.

Although I say *we,* and my husband *was* nearly as consumed with our daughter as I was, I couldn't help but notice that our parenting approaches played out quite differently. My husband didn't seem to have any problem compartmentalizing his role as father. He was mostly the same person he'd been before, except now he had a kid. But for me, everything had changed. I pretended to be the same, pretended to still care about things—like the rest of the world, and having fun, and having sex—but my interest wasn't real. I was like an actor, playing the pre-mom me in the made-for-TV movie of my life. I felt like I should've wanted to do something besides stare at my baby, so I said I did. I should've wanted to have sex, I believed, so I asked for it. Of course, I only asked in "safe" situations, like when I knew he needed to get up early for work, or right before the baby was due to wake. I was a master, really, at wanting it when it couldn't really happen, when I knew it wouldn't.

Ticket to the Moon

My husband is mad. His face is dark and intense as he pulls his jeans up over his softening erection. I'm naked, upset, and defensive, but also secretly relieved as he heads out of the bedroom, pissed. His anger takes sex off the table. I'm in the clear again, or at least skating on borrowed time. I don't know why he takes my lack of interest in sex so personally. "It's not you," I try to explain during our latest botched attempt at intercourse, "It's me." But my words come out sounding more like a high school breakup than an explanation, and my poor husband, embarrassed, hurt, and blue-balled, is furious. "Why did you start this," he asks, "when you never really wanted it? Don't even bother next time."

Good, I think to myself, getting up to check on the baby, *I won't.* I'm pissed now, too. Why did I start this? Because I mistakenly thought that he would be happier with pity sex than none at all. Because I could see how much he wanted it, how much he needed it. *Because I give a shit about our marriage, about being close again.* I started this because I thought I could fake my way through it and maybe, just maybe, even end up liking it. Contrary to popular belief around here, my husband isn't the only one who's freaked out by my total disinterest in sex. Since pregnancy, my libido is all over the map. It's up, it's down, and now it appears to be completely off the map, AWOL. I've heard that women hit their sexual peak in the early thirties. Okay: Here I am, libido, pushing thirty, ready to go. But nothing is happening. The engine is stalled. The battery is dead. Between postpartum hormones, nursing hormones, exhaustion, and overwhelming love for Ramona, I'm all shorted out.

"You know what I think?" my husband whisper-shouts from the other room (this is how we fight now, afraid of waking the baby, with whisper-shouts and furious gesticulating), and I have a feeling he's going to tell me whether or I want him to or not. "You don't like sex."

His words are venomous and it stings the way they hang there in that *There, I said it* kind of way. This is not what I meant to happen when I asked my husband to lie down with me, forty minutes of precious naptime ago. *It's not my fault,* I want to say. *I didn't make my breasts so sore and leaky. I can't help it.* I can't control my newly heightened sense of smell, or the fact that I'm repulsed by the scents he carries home from his workday: coffee, air-conditioning, meat sandwiches, smoke breaks he thinks I don't know about. I can't help worrying about my baby in the next room, about her rolling facedown or falling or choking or dying of SIDS. *It's not my fault,* I want to say, *that when you kiss me my instinct is to pat your back or lick your cheek, like you're my brother or son, or my yearling pup.*

The baby cries and I rush to pick her up; she's my shield, an easy out, the antidote to this whole nasty exchange. "Now look what you did," I say, putting up walls while I put her to my breast. "You woke the baby."

While it's debatable whether or not I've always liked sex, I've always liked the idea of it. There have been times when just thinking about my husband's naked knee between my legs is enough to make me cream. Before JB (and even with JB in our days before love and marriage and the baby carriage), for the most part, getting turned on was never a problem for me. I liked chasing down desire, and I had endless fun with the buildup to sex. It was the idea of someone wanting me that I found irresistibly hot, the tension of the moment *right before.* It was teetering on the precipice of ultimate intimacy with another person: the smell of his excitement, imagining what it would feel like to surprise him with a kiss, to lean over his body, to press my own against his, to feel the heat of that first physical connection. Back then, it was the follow-through that was the problem; the actual act left me feeling vulnerable and scared. As a teenager in the late eighties I knew that sex was messy and dangerous, but we all did it anyway—we just tried not to think too much about it. Even when I really liked a guy, even when things were safe and sweet, foreplay was still usually the best part. With the sex, I'd be so busy worrying about what the other person wanted, or how I looked, or whether or not I would come, that I'd blink and he'd be done. But I'd always go back for the buildup, for the anticipation of a first look, a kiss, a touch. The excitement for me was in the flirting, the teasing, the moment I knew I'd find myself skin to skin with a new body.

For JB and me, the act itself is the easy part; it's clean and sound and safe. We have years of physical communication under our belts, so our sex is almost always good. He knows how to touch me, he knows what I like, we know how to move. But now, getting turned on is the hard part. The wanting is what I can't get a grip on, and my total lack of desire is causing all this trouble. Maybe he's right; maybe I really *don't* like sex. Maybe that part of my life has gone the way of all-night parties and sleeping in. Maybe sex is just biologically incompatible with motherhood—too many hormones, too much touch. Maybe I have become some kind of frigid freak who can just live without it. But I don't want to live without it; I like the

But I don't want to live without it; I like the idea of **WANTING SEX.**

idea of wanting sex. I like thinking there's still a naughty side to me, to us. I'm still interested in at least having the *ability* to be interested.

My husband's sexual appetite is, on the other hand, totally intact. He is always on; his default state of existence is "horny." I could be covered in mush, insane, snappy, bitchy, bloated, stinky, or funky, and he's still ready to go. I swear, he even hit on me in the delivery room the day our daughter was born. Something about my robe.

The truth is, I need sex these days about as much as that famous need a woman has for a man: like a fish needs a bicycle. If he is "always on," sexually speaking, I am "always off." My default state of existence is "mommy," and unlike my husband I can't weed that out from other parts of myself. The role has taken me over like a plague, pushing out all other aspects of me. I try to care about—heck, even think about—other things, to focus on something besides my baby, but nothing else really interests me. I'm swimming in a world of maternal preoccupation. I'm a victim of biology. I'm twitterpated.

Nobody told me motherhood would change me this much. I find myself wondering if I'm normal. I wonder if my mom was right—always an unsettling thought—when she said that letting the baby sleep with us would be a surefire passion-killer. I wonder about other mothers' sex lives, about the women in my new moms' group who seem to have everything under control. Surely they're all having more sex than me. I imagine them swinging from chandeliers in their perfectly clean houses, their perfect, angelic children innocently napping upstairs. I wonder about my lesbian mom friends and their libidos. Do they ever have sex without a man in the house pushing for it? I certainly wouldn't. I imagine being married to a woman; how tidy things would be. We could bask in simple, gentle camaraderie, floating in low-testosterone bliss where we don't fight the minute we have a childless moment. The stress of sex's *hows, whens,* and *wheres* not charging the air, or sitting in the room with us like a contrary third party.

I read somewhere that one reason new mothers lack interest in sex is that they feel "touched out." Certainly that might explain things; with a nursing baby attached to my breast all day I'm tired of being touched and pulled and scratched and stretched. And yes, there are even times when, despite my infatuation, I want to fling her off of me as if she were some parasitic bug. But mostly I just want the rest of the world and all other living creatures to leave the two of us alone so I can hold my daughter and count her toes and stare at her like a high school sweetheart. Forget being "touched out" though. These days it's more like I'm touched just enough, thanks.

The reality is that my daughter and I are binary stars

caught up in the gravity of a celestial dance. We are a galaxy of two. She's the center of my universe, everything else is distant and insignificant. Mother-love is not something I dabble in, try on, treat as a side dish. For me, it's everything. And my past isn't providing me with many distractions: I didn't give up a high-powered job to get here, didn't trade in a satisfying career or give up a passionate hobby. I don't have many friends tethering me to Life Before Baby; I left most of my good friends in Seattle when I headed to California at eighteen, depressed and confused, in search of a brighter life. The friends I do have here are childless. They still live in the city, still go out drinking and partying till dawn. We're on separate planets now.

But hello, what's this? A bump? A fold? A black hole? There's another star out here, one I've forgotten about: a third in our system, nearly disconnected in its long, uneven orbit. I can't see it, but I feel its unstable influence. We gravitate toward it, pass it in the night, but we are on different planes. I feel it getting farther and farther away, pulling less and less. I can't see where it's headed, but I sense that it's on its own path, heading straight into the dark chaos of the unattached world.

"*Goddammit,*" I think to myself. "*Can't he do anything right with her?*"

From the bath, I can hear the baby crying. My body is pulled toward her; my milk lets down and leaks into the tub in thick creamy swirls. I force myself to stay in the tub. *Wait a minute,* I remind myself, *before rushing in and taking over.* This is what the parenting books say: *Step back. Let your partner find his own way with the baby. Let him make his own mistakes.*

His mistakes. I've got a running list of *tsk-tsk*s I've held my tongue over: the time he got soap in her eyes, the time he held her too tight—no, that's too loose . . . no, like *this!* And there was the time, ten days into things, when he almost sat on her. *I forgot she was there,* he said, crying after he'd nearly squashed her, plopping his giant man-booty down on the couch just millimeters from her face. He was so upset that I laughed it off and gently teased him about it later, but it still stuck with me, like the time his diapering job had been pinching her thigh.

Dealing with him, I'm the queen bitch, the angry mama bear, the boss of **ALL THINGS BABY.**

The problem isn't that he's incompetent. It's that I'm overcompetent. Fueled by hormones and pheromones, I'm focused completely on her needs in a way that he isn't. Dealing with him,

I'm the queen bitch, the angry mama bear, the boss of all things baby. She is my tiny captain: *Change your diaper? Yessir! Need a breast? I'm on it! Shall we dance? Indeed. You lead, I'll follow.* Our tango of attachment is intimate, passionate, exclusive. We meld, and our boundaries blur. I can't imagine, not even for an instant, forgetting she was there. Would I forget my heart? Would I forget to breathe?

I feel sorry for my husband. His love for Ramona is, at this point, mostly unrequited. He holds, kisses, coos, and cuddles, but ultimately he is challenged by his lack of breasts. Our daughter tolerates him, even throws him a gassy smile here and there, but her heart and body belong to me. The nursing—and the fact that I'm the one who's home with her all day—isn't the only thing that has snowballed her affections in my favor. It's something deeper, something instinctual. She knew my smell before she knew any others—my pulse, my voice, my warmth. For nine long months, more than half of her current existence, her dad wasn't really even in the picture.

Coming out of the bathroom, I turn the corner and watch from the hallway, dripping. JB sits at the edge of the bed, holding our daughter in his two giant hands, which are outstretched as if he were offering crudités on a platter to no one in particular. He's just staring at her, unmoving, unflinching, watching; he watches as her cries escalate and her tiny arms and legs thrash. He doesn't pull her close or try to comfort her—he doesn't move or make a sound.

"What are you doing?" I ask, trying to keep the judgment from my voice, but knowing full well it's coming out flat and pissed-off sounding anyway.

Suddenly I notice lines on my husband's face I don't recognize. I can see the desperation he feels at wanting to comfort her and somehow not being able to. I see a pain in him I haven't seen in years. For the first time in months, I actually see him. He looks up with sad, tired eyes and answers, "I think I need some help."

My husband is a complicated man with a complicated past. After he struggled to steer himself and his brother away from the dead end he saw looming in their future, when his brother landed in prison JB responded by permanently giving up on his own big dreams. He dropped out of college and took a furniture-moving job that required nothing but a body from him; there, no one knew about or had any interest in his beautiful mind. Around this time, he also met me.

By the time I got pregnant, years later, he'd begun opening himself to dreams again. Small, unassuming dreams, but dreams nonetheless. He had made a career for himself (computer programmer? Sure, why not?), married me (another excellent choice), and finally stopped trying to save his family (think: *Titanic*). And then our daughter was born and it blew him out of the water, the love he had for her, the big beautiful shameless dreams he had for her. I think, in a way, he thought her birth would fundamentally change him: Maybe fatherhood would destroy his personal demons and somehow make everything right.

At first, his life *was* different. We were both totally caught up in the miracle of her. Taking care of her needs focused us constantly on the immediate present; we lived in permanent high gear. But once things settled down, once he returned to work and I became the baby expert, life went more or less back to normal for him. He was spending three-quarters of his day with the same people, the same projects, and the same dumb email jokes as before. "Father" did not change him the way "Mother" transformed me. The new role was a bonus for him, an addition, an upgrade, but it didn't change who he was, didn't take him over or destroy his personal demons. It didn't make everything right. It was the same life, plus this, minus that. And, as I drifted farther and farther away from his dimming star on my mommy track, minus me.

He's been hiding that from me. He, too, had drifted back into the comfort of living life only as a series of basic requirements to be met. *I will maintain a house for my kids. I will keep a job for my kids. I will stay sane for my kids.* He was good at this life. It was safe and easy. It took the littlest amount of effort, the tiniest dreams. It was *just enough.* But on this day, as he sits alone—depressed, disengaged, and unhinged—with our daughter, helplessly holding her as she screams, he realizes it is going to take more than that *just enough* to be a good father, and to be the man he always wanted to be.

Our doctor is an asshole.

"Some guys can hack it; some just need a little extra help." That's what he's telling my shame-filled husband while writing a prescription for antidepressants. Because JB didn't feel weak and emasculated enough already, I guess.

We have all come to the doctor—me, my husband, our daughter, and her endless gear. On the drive home, Ramona naps. I put my hand on my husband's thigh and realize how long it's been since I touched him on purpose.

I remind my husband about the day that same doctor confirmed our pregnancy with a blood test. We were so nervous, excited and cautious and wound full of dreams, that every time a car sped, dangerously fast, past us, my husband would shake his fist at it and yell, "Baby on board, motherfucker!" As we talk I suddenly realize how much is at stake, how much he is investing in these two fussy women who want nothing to do with him. He is willing to sacrifice his hard-fought sense of independent, "man-need-no-help" masculinity in order to fight for us, for the sake of true paternity. He doesn't want to be emotionally-shut-down dad, he doesn't want to be good-enough dad. He wants to be Baby on Board dad, excited dad, engaged dad. He's hunting down fulfillment and happiness, gambling everything on love, and betting on the fact that *all that we are, and all that we have,* is more than enough. His devotion inspires me to fight for something, too. I'm determined to get the two of us back on track, to throw off this fog and start finding the pieces of our old life, our old love.

In the shower, I think I hear the baby crying. I turn off the water and drip, shivering, listening. It's quiet. I turn on the water again and shave my legs; it's been so long, it takes two of my husband's blades. We're leaving the baby for the first time tonight. A good friend, a teacher in the infant room of the last childcare center I worked at, has finally convinced us to let her take Ramona and to go out for a couple of hours *by ourselves.* As much as I hate the idea, I can tell it's time. My husband and I have been acting like brother and sister, or coworkers chatting as we change shifts, and I hate it. And despite any false hopes I may have had about the potential side effects of his antidepressant (a woman can dream, can't she?) Weeks later, I can't pretend not to notice that my husband remains up to his usual full sexual speed. I can see that he's getting tired of begging for the scraps of physical intimacy I occasionally throw his way.

Walking to the restaurant, we hold hands and check the cell phone way too many times. JB looks at me and wonders out loud if the baby will be asleep when we get home. I raise my eyebrows, trying to remember how to flirt with him. I try to say something naughty, but it falls flat and I end up instead nervously recounting some piece of news I heard on the radio earlier that day. As much as I *want* to want to be naughty, I really don't. What I want most is to rush home and kiss my baby.

As much as I want *to want to be naughty, I really don't. What I want most is to rush home and* **KISS MY BABY.**

We order drinks and food and sit outside on the covered patio, listening to music and watching the outdoor pool table. It reminds me of a trip we took to Mexico, not long before we decided we'd try to get pregnant. We spent hours sitting under umbrellas on the beach in Acapulco, talking and nursing our buckets of beer and people-watching. We were so high on sun and awesome vacation-sex that when a man selling drugs offered us a "ticket to the moon," we just shook our heads and laughed. We were already there, man; the two of us were blasting through life, heading into unknown territory while the rest of the world ate our dust. But that was then, this is now: Now, I've got a new copilot. It's my daughter I'm floating through life with, and JB is just sad debris that's getting left behind.

We watch some college students come out to smoke and flirt with the girls sitting at the table next to us. All of them are wasted, and before long they're flirting with us, too. My husband convinces me to play pool; I'm self-conscious and extremely out of practice, but for half an hour I actually almost forget about the baby. Before we leave, the students invite us to join them for a hot tub party. We laugh. It's so absurd I'm almost tempted. After two beers I'm tipsy myself. It's the most alcohol I've had in over a year. We show them pictures of our baby on the way out. They can't believe we have a kid; sometimes I can't either. Their surprise is a compliment; we might be old and boring (read: thirty and parents) but at least we don't look it. We say our goodbyes and pay our bill. It's time to turn back into pumpkins and head home.

On the way home, we stop at the video store. On a whim, I pull JB into the adult section and we browse the titles, laughing at some, raising eyebrows at others. I hang on JB's shoulder like I'm drunk, as if we just met and he's taking me home for a night of naughtiness. I feel the guy at the counter watching us; we're loud and obnoxious. I like the way he has no idea I'm a mom. He blushes when I set an erotic video on the counter and stare at him, keeping my eyes on his while he rings it up.

At home, our daughter is not only still alive, but sleeping peacefully on my friend's chest. "She took a bottle, then slept the whole time," she whispers, handing me the baby and gathering her things. "She was just fine." We thank her and send her home with a piece of chocolate cake and a nice bottle of wine. I plop onto the couch with the baby, breathing in her face, kissing her dimpled hands.

My husband hovers over the VCR, trying to get it to work. By the time the grainy video begins to play, I'm done. I lie on the couch with the baby, and pretend to be asleep. I hear my husband sigh, and pause the video. "Let's get you guys into bed," he says, helping us off the couch and into the bedroom, where he kisses my cheek and tucks me in before retreating back into the living room.

In bed, with the threat of sex gone, I fantasize about my husband dying; it's tragic, yes, for him to go so young, but at least we won't fight about sex anymore. At least I can just fall into complete absorption with my daughter. *Just the two of us; we can make it if we try.* . . . I picture us at the zoo together, the park, the video store. The video store. Suddenly I can't help but flash to the blushing indie clerk, to the sly, shy smile he slipped me as I walked out the door. Of course, as a grieving widow, I will have lost all my baby weight. I'll look desperate and thin, and he will corner me in the back of the store, and I'll be so weak with grief I'll have to let him take me, right there between *Raiders of the Lost Arse* and *Cafe Flesh.*

Ah-ha—what's this? A curious visit from my old cohort, my baffling buddy, my long-lost libido? It may not quite be all-systems-go, and my arousal leaves almost as quickly and inexplicably as it came, but it's a start, a step, a clue. Maybe it's not simply the idea of sex I don't like these days. Maybe it's the idea of sex with my husband that I have a problem with.

BUILDUP

SIX–EIGHTEEN MONTHS

SEXHAUSTION

CHAPTER 2

Q: How do you get a woman
to stop having sex with you?
A: You marry her.
—ANONYMOUS

Although mother-love is the prime suspect behind my lost libido, I'm looking at marriage as a close second. I doubt that in a lineup I could point to one over the other. They're both shady characters, likely in cahoots. The glimpse of libido I had after our porn-rental adventure was brief, and it hasn't been seen again. My dreams of naughty encounters with video-store clerks have been replaced by dreams of my daughter turning into a soft white kitten. I try to hold her, but she keeps shrinking and slipping away from me. I tighten my grip and she turns into a tiny seed that I lose on a dirty floor.

It's hard to believe that JB and I can't get it together to get together. Sex used to be our second language. Now it's second fiddle to everything else. The day after our wedding, in the summer of 1998, my husband and I were at the center of our own sexual universe. We were so consumed with each other, we even canceled our Las Vegas honeymoon and spent two weeks hiding out at home having "Oh my god, we're married" sex. The excitement of being married was enough for us; we sat in our sunny Berkeley backyard staring at each other, we went out for breakfast and admired our rings as we waved over a waitress or held hands across the table. We didn't need to go anywhere or do anything to celebrate. If we had, we wouldn't have left the hotel room anyway; we barely left our bedroom.

But just a couple weeks later, it was another story. In some ways, getting married changed everything. In some ways, it changed nothing. After the initial excitement and romance wore off, we were the same people, with the same arguments and the same life we had before, only, except, *forever.* Tacking that *forever* on there suddenly made those same arguments a lot more urgent: *Uh, hello, we're in this forever. We better figure this stuff out RIGHT NOW.* We fought like crazy for two months before eventually mellowing out and getting into our married-life groove, but even that, after being together for five years, wasn't exactly Las Vegas–life. It wasn't exactly thrilling.

Here's another confession: Even before the baby came, my husband and I may have had a fight or two about sex. Okay, maybe three. The dulling nature of marriage snuck up on us; we went from incredibly hot to pleasantly comfortable to way too comfortable nearly overnight. The fact that we could have body-blowing sex any time we wanted turned it from an indulgent dessert into instant mashed potatoes. And I like instant mashed potatoes—just not every day. I'm also a pickier eater than my husband; I'd rather just not eat than have potatoes *again.* Not wanting to be the one to starve us, though, I would arrange fancy dinner dates, buy fancy lingerie, and, yes, even bring home guides like *101 Nights of Grrreat Romance.* The night I brought that book home we pored over it, dog-earing the pages that looked interesting. And then days passed, and the book got shoved aside and buried under dirty laundry, or homework from a class one of us was taking, or the clothes we stripped off each other after drinking too much wine and doing grrreat romance the way we used to. Weeks later, the book made it to the bookshelf in the basement, along with our dusty old copy of *8 Minutes in the Morning to a Flat Belly* or *Buns of Steel: Total Body Workout.* Because really, there's no magic recipe, no store-bought insta-romance, no quick fix for romance any more than there's a quick fix for killer abs or a great ass. It's work. And although we were still much hungrier for each other than we would be a couple years later, we hated the idea that *we* would ever have to work at it. It just didn't make sense. Work at it? Us? We used to have to work at *not* doing it all the time, rousing each other out of bed to live the lives that didn't stop just because time seemed to when we were together. Work at it? When I used to blush just thinking about him? When he used to shake with anticipation before even touching me?

WORK AT IT? US?

We used to have to work at not *doing it all the time . . .*

Before long, though, the lack of romance became a non-issue. My pregnancy filled us with a new kind of romantic excitement, bringing us closer together in a new way. Our sex life wasn't what it once was, sure, but heck, I had a little person growing inside me. A little version of us!

Furthermore, once we got past the first trimester and all that vomiting, we eased into a new sex groove. My husband's libido, I've discovered, is pretty much ready and raring to go no matter what, including pregnancy. That second trimester was probably the only time in our sexual history, besides the first couple of months we spent together, that our libidos truly matched, that we were on the same sexual page. I was flush and fat with extra blood and juices. At night I would have crazy sex dreams in which my husband, hung like a fertility statue, would plunge deep inside me until I could feel him all the way in my chest. Pregnancy made me dream like a guy. No plot, no other characters, just straight penetration. Normally my sex dreams are the other way around: all plot, all buildup, not much actual sex. I'd wake up from these new dreams satisfied in a way I hadn't been before. And then, for good measure, I'd wake up my husband and get the same satisfaction in real time. I was motivated by a deep, primal drive that felt out of my control. Maybe second-trimester sex is nature's way of keeping us from being simply a maternal depository—a way to make our men happy so they stick with us through the whole damn thing.

In the third trimester I got big and anxious and uncomfortable, and our sex life swung the other way. I cared more about nesting than sex, but we'd find creative ways to do it now and then—for him. My husband never complained, or took the rejection personally. My lack of interest didn't affect his self-esteem or anything else. He just took it in stride and figured it was par for the pregnancy course, part of the deal. He could wait it out.

And now, after all that waiting, six months have passed since I gave birth. And? Nothing. Not a blip of arousal on my radar screen. He's completely confounded by my lack of libido.

He can't conceive of the fact that I can physically have sex, but don't want to. To him, it's simple. Sex feels good. You're a woman; I'm a man; there's the bed. What's the problem? But sex is anything but simple to me; my desire for it is still mysteriously missing, leaving only a foggy vacancy in that department, and I don't know how to explain it to him. There are myriad theories that could justify it—exhaustion, breastfeeding, hormones—but they aren't the same as a clear reason.

Now, when I say "No," or "Please don't touch me, you're making my skin crawl," he takes it so personally. "No means no" he knows, of course. But coming from me, "No" also means something else to him. Something like "I don't like you," or "I don't care about your needs." But I do. I love my husband more than ever, in fact. Sitting next to him, staring at the best thing we've ever done together, I swell. But not down there—down there I'm still flat and empty. Down there the mystery continues, and to avoid fighting with him about it or hurting his feelings, I sometimes have sex when I don't really want to. The rest of the time, I avoid any touch or talk that might give him the wrong impression, and I use the excuse built conveniently into having a new baby: *I'm too tired.*

It's no lie. I am, in fact, exhausted. I knew that having a baby would be a lot of work and that I'd miss some precious shut-eye, but I had no idea how physically demanding it would be. My body is starting to revolt, leaving me feeling much more "knotty" than "naughty." I don't think there's one part of me that's physically unaffected by pregnancy or childbirth. Everything is tired and sore. My breasts are alien: They're now huge, balloony sacks that are miraculously sensitive and desensitized at the same time. Running is out of the question—my boobs would be a hazard to me and anyone within a block radius. (*Cla-clunk, cla-clunk.* "Run for your life! They're coming!" *Cla-clunk, cla-clunk.*) They hang low; they wobble to and fro. I could throw them over my shoulder like a continental soldier.

My nipples, which used to be a shortcut to arousal, are now a for-sure shortcut to "What the hell are you thinking?" My butt, once a safe haven, known to enjoy a nice little slap here and there, has also suffered. It's so wrong, especially since I had a C-section and didn't actually push anything out, but there they are: hemorrhoids, keeping the magic of that special time alive. I know I'm supposed to feel like a beautiful, fertile mother-goddess, but most days I feel more like the Green Goddess salad dressing at my favorite dive restaurant: lumpy, watered down, and terribly overused.

Even my teeth have been affected by motherhood. When I go to the dentist for a painful popping and clicking I've developed in my jaw, he tells me I have symptoms of a problem with my temporomandibular joint, or TMJ. "We see a lot of moms with this," he says, filling a mold with plastic that will help me stop clenching and grinding my teeth at night. "It will help if you can get some rest." *Get some rest. No shit,* I think, clenching and grinding away my barely suppressed anger. I have a sudden urge to pick up the ceramic mold of my mouth and break his perfect teeth with it. I hate him for telling me what I already know—that is, until he instructs me to avoid big yawns and other such activities that might have me opening my mouth wider than usual, where it could get stuck. Suddenly he's forgiven. There's my free pass, my doctor's note, my get-out-of-jail-free card; blowjobs are now officially out of the question.

There's my doctor's note, my get-out-of-jail free card; blowjobs are now officially **OUT OF THE QUESTION.**

My husband is a kind, sensitive, and very generous lover. His prowess has nothing to do with my own evaporating drive. But sometimes he's too kind, too sensitive. He takes it as a personal affront if I don't reach orgasm, if I'm not screaming in ecstasy each time we make love. He doesn't get how his generosity has become just another burden, that too often I see his erect penis as a soldiering drill sergeant, demanding: "Hup, two, three, four! I am just another chore!" He can't see that I'm so adrift in my own Madonna and Child afterglow that I've completely put sex out of my mind; that I'm satisfied in a deeper way than even the best sex can produce. He doesn't get where I'm coming from when I say that sexual satisfaction isn't that important to me right now—that I'm fine with doing it just for him sometimes, and it doesn't have to be a big deal. These days, sex is always a big deal.

"So," my husband drawls incredulously, when I'm trying to explain some of this to him during a naptime sex session that's quickly going awry, "you're basically saying that you want me to masturbate inside of you? You don't actually want to be *involved*?"

The hurt in his voice makes me start backpedaling. "No, it's not that. . . . I mean, okay, it is that, but what's so wrong with having it be just *for you* sometimes?" I try to sound coy, hiding my obsession with the clock behind his head: *tick tock tick tock*. I can hear precious naptime ticking away. It's clear I won't be crossing "Be sex goddess" off my über-housewife/Supermom to-do list for today. *Why can't he just RealDoll me and get it over with?* I think. *Damn.*

My husband gives me a look, then rolls heavily off my naked body. "You're a liar," he says as he pulls up his jeans. He's not saying it maliciously, but he's also not hiding his disappointment and brewing anger. "You say you want sex, but you don't." This, right here, is one reason it's not easy for me to tell him no. This is the fight we always end up back at. I close my eyes in defensive frustration and wish I could say something to make it all better. It's technically true that I didn't *want* sex this afternoon. But I totally wanted to *have had* sex this afternoon.

Maintaining our fragile romantic connection is yet another chore on my ever-growing list. It's like our houseplants: My husband doesn't ever think to water them. He doesn't notice their brittle leaves, or the way they droop and sag and get pale. But he likes having them around as much as I do. He likes the way they make our house feel fresh and alive. If I didn't water them, they'd die, no doubt about it; by the time he noticed they weren't doing well, it would be too late. I don't want our relationship to wilt away, so I seek out connection in the one sure way I know to get it from him, through sex. We've always connected this way: When he doesn't have words, or can't tell me what he's feeling, he shows me. It's an important anchor for him. Doing it this afternoon would have made us close and tender all weekend. It would have opened him up to me, and let him show me things he doesn't know how to say.

On top of that—and I know my liberal feminist parents would be horrified to hear me say this—I have this archaic belief that somehow sex is one of my wifely, stay-at-home duties. I'm not afraid my man will stray or leave me if he doesn't get any; I simply want him to be happy, and I hate the idea of letting him down. I hate the idea of not being the perfect housewife-mother-lover.

My relationship to feminism has always been a little rocky. Growing up in the late seventies and early eighties, I was told by my parents and teachers that I could do or be anything I wanted to. I watched my mom fight to make that dream a reality for me, to make the world a better place for me, so I could have the equality and opportunities she didn't have. She lived much of her life in reaction—to a society that told her the pinnacle of her career would be as a telephone operator, to people around her who didn't see how much she really deserved to get out of life. Armed with the newly won freedoms of her time, my mother devoted herself to inoculating me and other girls in my generation against the shame, timidity, and sexist expectations she had grown up with. She led us in assertiveness training courses and Aikido classes, she spoke freely of sex and spirituality, she fought for and modeled all kinds of strong independence. But I think she also stretched herself too thin; she gave too much of herself and paid for it with divorce, depression, and distance from the people who mattered most to her.

And then, of course, there's me. By the time I got pregnant, the choice for me to stay at home was an easy one. At-home motherhood was better (though on the surface, not always terribly different) than any of the jobs I had before: taking care of other people's kids, doing other people's laundry, washing other people's dirty dishes. With this job there were no awful "ice-breaking" exercises, no fluorescent lights, no long commute. And fortunately my husband makes good money, likes his job, and is happy to support us (although he does say that it will be his turn to stay home when our daughter is two: "You get the first two years, I get the second two," he says, but I don't think he realizes just how much money he makes, or how little I would make going back to being a preschool teacher). In some ways, I'm certain that I could be or do anything I wanted to; it's just that all I've ever really wanted was what I felt I missed growing up. I wanted chocolate, dammit, not carob. I wanted a nice, quiet house with a nice, quiet mom who was at home. I wanted more of the personal in my life, and less of the political.

And now's my chance. So over the past year I have taken on the role of homemaker with the gusto of the newly converted. But this Supermom thing is harder and more confusing than I thought it would be, and it's not exactly libido lifting. All this putting out—food, milk, physical attention, holding, nursing, rocking, wrestling, love, excitement, encouragement, patience—makes putting out, in the high school sense, just not a priority. And it's not just my sex drive that's suffering. Desperate to be the perfect mom and the perfect wife, I'm losing touch, losing my grip, and paying a price I can't see yet.

Although I would never trade these sun-filled days at home with my daughter for anything, they're certainly not easy. I'm overwhelmed with responsibilities and tasks: clean the house, pay bills, keep the baby alive and healthy, maintain adult relationships, maintain my sanity, walk the dogs. I'm not naturally a domestic diva (my cute vintage-looking apron says Crafty and Sexy, when really I'm neither), but I'm trying. For years, our couch was nothing but a piece of foam on the floor covered by an old sheet. Now not only do we have an actual couch, but I'm aware I've been mistakenly using the word "curtains" when I really meant "window coverings." I make elaborate sandwiches to send off to work with my husband. I buy and cook fresh organic vegetables so they're soft enough for my daughter to mash with her two tiny front teeth. Of course, most days I forget to feed myself, and even if I do remember or notice that I'm hungry, I can't seem to find the time or inclination to do anything about it.

This Supermom thing is harder than I thought it would be, and it's not exactly **LIBIDO LIFTING.**

Maybe this new gung-ho domesticity is my newest way of rebelling, like the time in high school when I told my mom casually over breakfast that I would never call myself a feminist and waited for her reaction. "Oh, honey," she said. "What about the sacrifices we made? The work? The movement?"

"Right," I said, hitting her up on the way out for lunch money to buy cigarettes with. "But it worked, okay? If someone tried to tell me I couldn't do something because I'm a girl, I'd just say 'Fuck you' and do it anyway. See? You don't have to worry. It, like, totally worked. I don't need to be a feminist."

I've developed a somewhat better understanding of the subject since then, of course; at the time I was angry, and wanting to push her buttons. I hated feminism because I blamed it for stealing my mom away from me when I was a scared, confused kid and I needed her. I hated it for driving her to hang out with butchy lesbians and other loud, angry women, instead of with me at home. I hated that her vocabulary had started to include words like "erotic" and "sensual" and "passion." I wanted for her to only be passionate about the life she had, the one I could see her shedding a little bit more of each day, as if it were the dried snakeskin and leaf-skeletons that subtly decorated the fresh paint on the walls of her quiet new apartment. She was growing out of that life, though, the same way I had outgrown my imaginary friend and my favorite red shoes and my love of horses. As a kid I wanted so desperately for that old life to be enough for her, because that life was the one I knew. We were in that life together all the time, not just every other weekend or on Wednesday nights.

In some ways I feel like I'm still fighting for my mom's attention and closeness. That's how I ended up in California, following her move from Seattle after I dropped out of my fancy liberal arts college. Now, even though she's only twenty minutes away from our home in Berkeley, it's still hard to find time for each other. She has a framed card in her foyer reading Grandma's My Name, Spoiling's My Game, but she's also got her own busy life. She's not the classic gray-haired, knitting, retired matriarch of old. As the president of her own company, she works like crazy—taking business trips, putting in long hours, working on the weekends. When we do get together she spoils Ramona and me rotten; she buys toys and ice cream for my daughter, and new non-mom-looking bras and underwear for me.

And now here I am, throwing myself heart and soul into a reaction, in much the same way my mom did with her feminist work. The direction may be different, but the destination is a little too close for comfort. I'm swinging on the other far side of the pendulum. As a kid, feminism looked to me a lot like leaving: freedom from family, long hours at work. It looked like "out there" instead of "in here." So here I am, all about "in here." I can sense that I'm taking it too far, but it's so sticky and safe-feeling I don't want to pull myself out. It's my own new feminism, and no one can call me on it—not even my mom or my husband—because this is my choice, even when I know I have others. Because I am as sure as the giant milk-filled boobs on my chest that I am by far the most qualified person to stay at home with my daughter.

I've become almost like an addict; if romantic relationships were my intimacy fix before, these ten-hour days alone with the baby are my new drug of choice. I'm mainlining now, just a step away from ODing, and I've got the personal hygiene to prove it: I'm stinky, saggy, shaggy. I can't comb my own hair, but I groom every inch of my daughter with slow care. I'm high as a kite, totally blissed out. My world revolves around maintaining my fix; my world revolves around her. I'm stunted and dumb, primitively satisfied: a born breeder: "Me have purpose. Me make baby. Me HAPPY." I'm a throwback to the dark ages, I'm overwhelmed by ancient instincts and hormones: gather, tend, listen, protect, prepare, cover, warm, repeat. . . . *What about this? What about that?* My senses of sight, sound, and smell are heightened, on constant alert. I've become a master multitasker.

But multitasking, useful as it is for parenting, isn't the best mindset for sex. It's yet another player in the desire doldrums. "Relax," my husband whispers as I let him have sex with me. *Hmmm.* I think. *Relax.* I can't relax because I'm not wet at all, because I'm worried the condom will break, because I don't know what to make for dinner, because I bounced another check, because I think I hear the baby waking up in the next room, because I'm exhausted, because even though I've already told him which body parts are off limits his hands keep wandering in search of my magic button, because I knew from the beginning I wasn't going to come, because . . . good lord, how long can this take?

As physically exhausting as mothering is, it's the mental exhaustion of this unending multitasking that really wears me out, that really takes its toll. It is exhausting to always be preparing, protecting, pontificating on my daughter's well-being, to constantly be on high alert, in threat assessment. Stuck in survival mode, I assess the physical threats lurking everywhere: SIDS, choking hazards, falls, fevers, autism, rolls, suffocation, feral four-year-olds at the park. Then there are the choices, dozens of them daily, that will surely influence the rest of my daughter's life, that will undoubtedly etch in stone her course: Tap water or bottled? This pediatrician or that? Immunizations? Growth charts? Is she too fat? Too skinny? Is she happy enough? Smart enough?

I'm consumed with a frantic mother-fever that burns like instinct inside me, forcing everything else out, including my need for sex. *Hold on. Don't let anything slip. Hold tight, hold tight*. With so much noise I can't hear or focus on anything else. My mind moves nonstop, always racing, tripping several steps ahead of *now*. Despite his adoration for our daughter, my husband's focus is still clear and simple, primitively on-task: MMM. SEX GOOD. PUT SEED IN WOMAN. His mind isn't racing when we're twined together; you can bet he's not multitasking. I don't think he would notice, caught in the act, if the house were on fire. *Oh baby*, he'd say, still pumping away, flames lapping at his rear, *you're* so *damn hot*.

JB has always been a singularly focused man. He can do one, *maybe* two things at the same time. It's what makes him such a terrible driver, and what makes him such a good computer programmer. It's what made him so totally irresistible to me when we met: Everyone else in the world disappeared when he looked at me. Now, though, his focus seems to be on what he's not getting. These days, simply because he catches a glimpse of my nursing breast, or brushes against me, or, like, breathes, I'm supposed to turn all my instinct off, shut down my multitasking mind just like that, and get majorly turned on for a (maybe) twenty-minute (maybe) baby-free window of time.

I've always needed more than just a few minutes of opportunity or a naked visual to get turned on. I need time, finesse. I need Hallmark moments. Not the cheesy, prefab kind, but *our* kind, the kind we started with. I need him to pick me bright purple flowers from the neighbor's garden. I need poems, like the one he once scribbled on an old napkin and left on the kitchen table after a fight: *Your love is my sanity/Every day it rescues me.* Sure, naked body-rubbing followed by unhurried and gentle licking is nice, but emotional connection is an essential part of the buildup to sex for me—that's what gets my juices flowing, what tickles my fancy, what pleases my places. I need to hear him call me "Lover" and "Sweets" again. What happened to that? When did I stop being "Sweets"? When did I stop being "Lover"?

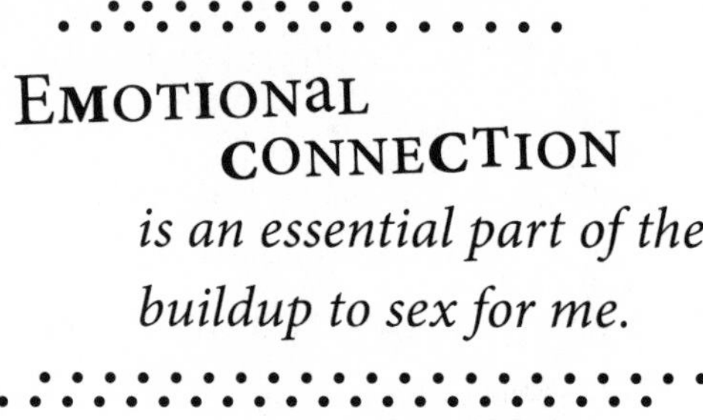

Pre-baby, I was the one who took care of most of the preliminaries. I didn't mind taking that on. I didn't mind being the one to buy erotic books or set up dates; he would always reciprocate with more than his fair share of romance and connection. But now, we're both too tired. We both give so much, physically and mentally, to our daughter that we have nothing left for each other. We're suffering from "sexhaustion." Getting it on is no longer spontaneous and easy and fun; it's something to feel guilty about, it's work, it's sit-ups. Who wants to do sit-ups when you're too tired to even talk? Who wants to eat when cooking takes up whatever's left of your energy? It's enough to make me lose my appetite altogether.

Well, most of the time.

I have, it turns out, developed quite an appetite for the man I've been seeing behind my husband's back. His name is Michael, and he's tall and thoughtful and incredibly fit; his muscular, ropy-veined forearms are obscenely attractive. With him, it's all dessert, it's never mashed potatoes. He brings me back into my body, backing me away from my multitasking mania by focusing strictly on me. He never complains and we never fight; he just gives it to me rough and impersonal like I've come to like it, and he expects very little from me in return. With Michael there is no work, no pressure, no messy emotions; we are strictly business. He knows what I need and he understands my body in a way my husband never could. With Michael I enjoy each minute because I know we're not going *there,* it's all buildup.

I'm hot for Michael. The problem is, other women are too, and right now we're all standing in line at the upscale pharmacy to sign up for his time in twenty-minute slots. I hold my breath as the woman in front of me miraculously wanders off, leaving me first on the list.

"She's asleep again," Michael says quietly, pointing to my daughter, crashed out in her leopard-print-lined stroller. "I know," I reply, feigning surprise—as if I didn't plan it, as if she didn't nap at this time every day, like clockwork—and climb onto his portable massage table. "I guess we're just meant to be."

Strolling home from my clandestine body work, I worry about my naughty little secret. I wonder why I haven't told my husband about it; there's nothing between Michael and me except the occasional twenty-minute midday table massage. And I'm not really sexually attracted to him, although I could be if I let myself. The way he works my body makes me feel quiet and comforted. It makes me feel cared about.

I'm surprised by how good it feels to be touched. With my husband I'm still so afraid of starting something I won't want to finish that I avoid anything that might vaguely be construed as sexual, or that could lead to sex. Hugging? Too close. Kissing? No way. Sitting on the couch watching TV? Well, mostly safe, but watch the feet. Massages are out of the question—my husband is incapable of rubbing any part of my body for more than three minutes without getting a hard-on (and it takes even less time if I have him use lotion). Even if that weren't an issue, the awkward, choppy thumbing he calls massage hardly counts as relaxing, and any direction I give him sets him off-task again. He takes any comment like "less spine" or "down a little" as just another invitation to grab my ass—he's so hungry for me, he's so starved for physical affection.

Even with nothing going on, my time with Michael feels guilty and splurgy; at twenty bucks a pop, massage to-go is not a cheap habit. I feel bad spending my husband's hard-earned money on something as extravagant as myself—why is it so hard for me to take a little something for myself and feel like I deserve it?

My husband, the feminist, would never call it his money. "Half of what I make is yours," he told me passionately the first time I tried to explain how weird it felt to not be contributing financially, how guilty I felt about even buying a new pair of pants when none of my old ones fit. Economic independence has been drilled into me in a way that leaves me feeling vulnerable and inadequate now that I'm not working. "But you *are* working," my husband says. "And you should get paid to stay at home, so just take half of what I make and call it yours."

I understand what he's saying in theory, but in reality I'm stuck in ye olden days. It's hard for me to think of what I do every day as work. Growing up I always thought I'd be an environmental lawyer, or a writer, or an astronaut—these were the kinds of things I was taught women should aspire to—not a *housewife.* And despite all the family-values rhetoric in this society, family work isn't valued; if it were I would at least be earning my own social security for these years spent at home with my kid. Mostly, though, it's hard for me to think of what I do as work because unlike most of my former jobs, I like what I'm doing. I get to go for long hikes in the middle of the day with the love of my life; I get to hang around the house in pajamas. I'm privileged and I know it—we can afford for me to stay home—and that, too, leaves me feeling bad if I let some part of this new gig slip. I feel lazy every time the baby naps and I watch TV instead of cleaning. I feel like I'm not contributing enough if we have to spend money on pizza again because I can't pull dinner together. And I feel guilty if a weekend or two comes and goes and we still haven't done it. I feel guilty each night that we crawl into bed and I turn my back and once again choose sleep over sex.

I'm starting to realize that I'm not the only one who makes that choice, or the only one with this guilt. The women in my new moms' group are getting more real, more honest. We're talking less about poop these days and more about the real shit we're all facing. I even fessed up about my lack of a sex life, making a disparaging joke about myself and my lack of need for it. The joke bombed, though, and the room became way too silent. I was just about to start glossing it over, diffusing my disclosure, when suddenly one woman broke the silence with a similar story. Within minutes everyone had a story to tell, a hushed confession about not wanting sex, or building resentments, or feeling guilty. "I thought I was the only one," one woman said, close to tears.

"I thought it was just me." But obviously it wasn't—otherwise, the trashy magazines I'd bought recently wouldn't have had articles for the modern mom with titles like "Having It All—Sleep *and* Sex" and "Sleep vs. Sex: You Don't Have to Choose." Um, hello—yes, we do. With forty-five minutes to three hours max of quiet me-time a day, I do have to choose. And I'm always going to choose sleep. I love sleep. Sleep is restorative, and simple, and I'm really good at it, no matter what else is going on in my life. Sex, on the other hand, is complicated, and involves other people. Its results are unpredictable. It requires work, and energy I don't have.

These days there's plenty of guilt to go around, and it sure sticks easily to those moms who don't feel up for sex. The media doesn't help any: Throw a dirty diaper and you'll hit a photo of a beautiful, glowing celebrity who's just had a baby. She has a great career—though it's presently on hold—and a better, sexier, bustier body than ever. Gorgeously attired in Versace or Valentino, she'll talk about mother-love and how much it's changed her life, but she also looks so good there's no possible way she's not having great, mind-blowing sex. Clearly, sexiness isn't work for her; it's a cinch, a snap. The moms on daytime TV commercials are superheroes as well, furthering the myth of this unattainable ideal: They are vessels of goodness, imbuing angelic infants with serenity and cherubic instruction. They are masterful cleaners and multitaskers, lovely and respectable-looking in matching coordinates. And they're just sexy and winky enough to let us know they're satisfying their men with plenty of hot married sex, too. I'm appalled by them, and I see right through them with my media-savvy self. I know they're neither real nor realistic—but damn it, I still want to be them. I want to be that perfect mother, be that perfect wife, make my man happy, *feel like a nat-ur-al woman*. But I guess I'm not buying the right detergent, because usually, I don't. Usually I'm just tired and downright uninterested in sex—and, of course, feeling guilty about it.

As things have it, my husband and I are going to be apart for our three-year wedding anniverary—eight years altogether, and our first anniversary since the baby. I have a family reunion in Spokane; the baby and I are going to head north a week early, the week of the anniversary, to visit friends and family in Seattle. My husband will meet us later, flying directly into Spokane for the reunion. I tell him we'll celebrate when we get back home, but secretly I'm relieved; I don't have to buy new underwear after all.

It's only a two-hour flight from Oakland to Seattle, and my daughter is perfect; she sleeps most of the time, charming other passengers in the short time she's awake. When my dad pulls over to pick us up, I realize how much I've missed him. I'm surprised at how adept at snapping and buckling carseats he is. But of course he would be: He lives with his wife (my stepmom) and my brother's family in the giant house we grew up in. He gets his grandpa fix every day, playing with my nephew, who's just two weeks older than my daughter.

It's great to be home. The cousins are so cute together: They have the same eyes, and their bald heads make them resemble their grandpa even more. My sister-in-law and I slip out for lattes and a bitch session while everyone else coos and caws over the babies. We have a lot to tell each other. We talk about sleeping patterns and how much coffee we'd like to drink as opposed to how much we should since we're both still nursing. We talk about larger issues, too: how we don't miss work or sex, and how our husbands work too much and do miss sex, and how we miss being alone but hate being away from our babies. Back at home, my gaggle of child-free childhood girlfriends swoops in and vies for holding time. *Come to Auntie Lex, let Auntie Chrissy hold you, Auntie Sara's turn now. . . .* I also didn't realize how much I've missed my friends, how much I've missed having people I love get to know my daughter and be part of this new life I've taken on. These are the girlfriends who screamed with me about first kisses and first times and put up with my bad boyfriends. As kids we logged hours planning our future lives: who we would end up marrying (or at least scamming with that weekend), how we would be famous, what we'd look like "old." We told each other everything, we wiped each other's tears and running mascara, and we backed each other up no matter what. In a lot of ways we raised each other in our own little boy-crazed, drama driven, unconditionally fun village. And now I wonder how I can raise my daughter without them. I wonder what the heck I'm thinking trying to do this so far away from home.

Over iced tea my friends fill me in on the latest insane dramas that constitute single life, detailing the high and low points of being thirty, as we all laugh and pass around the baby, amazed at how grown-up we've become. So many other people are doing all the work—feeding me, cleaning up, holding the baby—that before long the stubborn kink in my shoulder, the one Michael pinches and kneads so well, begins to loosen.

The next day I meet my girlfriends for coffee and shopping. To them, the baby is an irresistible accessory: They take turns showing her off, carrying her around as if she were theirs. They hold her while I try on new clothes, steer me away from the baggy comfortable kind I'm used to wearing, and bring me funky shirts that show off my new cleavage. I buy a couple, but can't imagine actually wearing them. Later, we pop into a restaurant and I run into a former boyfriend I've always liked. We've been friends for a long while, and I've long since forgiven him for the time I heard through the grapevine that he called me "boring in bed." (What can I say? I was. Of course, I was also nineteen and confused, and often quite wasted when we were together, but fair enough.)

I invite him to come up to my dad's place after work so we can catch up. He shows up at 9 PM with a six-pack of beer, and we sit in the backyard swapping gossip. He pounds four beers in the time I can sip two (and I can't even finish the second one). When my daughter wakes up and I nurse her, my friend doesn't know where to look; the fact that my breast is for nursing and no longer just for fun is still too weird to him. In many ways he's exactly the same guy he was ten years ago, but I'm definitely not the same girl. I've got living proof attached to my nipple. He finishes what's left of my second beer, and suddenly I'm ready for bed. All this beer and talk of old times has made me woozy, and nostalgic. "Why did we break up?" he asks, and I remind him that I cheated on him with his friend. "Oh yeah," he says, and laughs. I always felt bad about that; I was such a wreck back then. It feels good to finally say I'm sorry and mean it. With my daughter back asleep on the couch, I walk my friend to the door and we hug. He leans forward a little too much, feeling out if there's a kiss. For a second, I have an urge to prove to him I'm no longer boring in bed—to throw myself on top of him and wriggle all over, to stick my tongue down his throat and climb him like a cat on a scratching post. Instead I hug him again and kiss his cheek. Inside, I lean against the door and breathe. Where the hell did *that* come from? Why does the smallest bit of attention from any man but my husband result in spontaneously come-bustible thoughts? Bothered, I call my husband and tell him over and over how much I love him, how I can't wait to see him next week. Lyrics I thought I'd long forgotten from our early days together flood through me: a song he wrote in bed, on lined yellow paper, as we shared the afterglow: *pussycat want scratching post/carnivore want flesh/though I'm not the kind to boast/I'm sure I'll pass your test/pussycat want scratching post/heat want to be flame/flames that lick me till I roast/this cat feels the same.*

August in Spokane is *hot.* As soon as I check into the motel where the reunion is, I change into a crappy old swimsuit, the only one that fits, and head for the pool. My daughter loves the water. She laughs and splashes and tools around in her little baby-floater. After a couple hours she gets tired and I take her back to our room, where she nurses and we fall asleep together on one of the two queen beds in the air-conditioned room. I wake to knocking and my husband's voice on

HEARING HIM, *my stomach flips automatically, the way it did eight years ago.*

the other side of the door. Hearing him, my stomach flips automatically, the same way it did eight years ago. I wasn't expecting him until much later. He mumbles something through the door about missing us so much and catching an early flight. As nice as it's been to be back with my family and friends, and as much help as I've had, the truth is I've missed him terribly; he's still by far the best second-in-command. I throw open the door, forgetting for a minute that I'm naked, my wet swimsuit already dry on the floor where I left it.

Without saying anything, my husband pushes me into the small dressing area of our room and lifts me up onto the waist-high counter across from the closet that doubles as a full-length mirror. Amazingly, I'm excited by his force, by the way he drops his pants without taking his eyes off me. Motels have always been good to us. I think back to one trip we took, how in a frenzy we moved the mirrored vanity to accommodate our play, how the next day we giggled at the note the housekeeper left: *Please don't move the furniture.*

I'm just starting to relax into things and like the idea of this when I catch myself in the mirror, my worn and strangely redistributed new body looking back at me like a joke. As much as I appreciate all the work my body has done for me, I hardly consider it sexy. It has all the charm of a dull, nicked-up tool. Is a hammer sexy? A lawnmower? I'm utilitarian now: carry, bend, nurse, repeat. Carry, bend, nurse . . . The distraction is disheartening, and my multitasking mind jumps into action: *Did someone say nurse? Where's the baby? How long will she sleep? What if she wakes up? Is this really worth it?* I'm losing my focus, my interest is waning.

My husband senses what's happening, but instead of giving up or getting mad, or distracted himself, he turns off the light and walks me to the other queen bed, laying me down. He kisses me and whispers "Happy anniversary" somewhere between my ear and my neck. I shiver. He gets up and stacks a row of pillows next to our sleeping daughter on the other bed, creating a soft wall so we can't see her and she can't see out or roll onto the floor. He comes back to our bed and climbs on my back, straddling me naked. He starts rubbing my back, my shoulders, my arms. He's controlled and thoughtful, studying my skin, my tired muscles, a mole he hasn't seen before. The pressure of his body on top of me pushes me into the cool motel sheet and trips a wire. I'm focused now. I don't want to fake this one; I don't want to fight about it, or for it to be just *for him.* I want it for me, for us, for what we had and hopefully what we still have. Lost sensation floods through me, and the next time he rubs me I push back into him, our naughty parts communicating our heat and sweat and excitement. He kisses my back and I suck in my breath as he turns me over. He's no dummy now, he completely avoids my breasts, but keeps kissing everywhere else until I can't tell sweat from spit from my own warm wetness. "Eight years, wife," my husband says. It's just the two of us again, the way that we were before, in any old motel or car or alleyway. This is the thrill I'm looking for, the connection, the key to my lost libido. I think for a moment about trying to document this, to fingerprint this moment, to put it in my easy-access files or bribe it to stay somehow. I worry about losing sight again of what this experience is like—about it disappearing around a corner or going up in a cloud of smoke. But then I feel my husband inside me, on top of me, all around me. I feel him watching me, having me, loving me in that same singular way he always has, and suddenly I let go of thinking altogether; it's far too much work.

Fault Lines

CHAPTER 3

[D]on't expect to have sex if you aren't doing your fair share of the childcare and housework. While you've probably never considered vacuuming and taking the garbage out to be romantic acts, good luck getting laid without doing these sort of things once the new baby arrives.

—PAUL JOANNIDES, *The Guide to Getting It On! America's Coolest and Most Informative Book About Sex*

Thirty hours after giving birth, a truth of motherhood hit me like a Mack truck. Lying there, sliced open from the C-section, breasts hard as barnacled rocks, I woke up seconds before our newborn daughter cried to eat. Unable to sit up and lift her out of her bassinet, I called to my husband, who had finally just fallen asleep. He woke up delirious, exhausted from staying up with us through the night. "I've hit a wall," he cried. "I can't do it. I just can't do it."

"*Can't do it?*" I thought. "*Hit a wall?*"

Can't do it has no place in motherhood. It is a nonthought. Even thirty hours into the gig, I knew that. I said nothing, and he brought me the baby. I remember wondering how our marriage would ever survive. I remember wondering how any married couple survives having kids.

Life After Baby is rocky. For us, Sex After Baby is more so; first we're as close as two people can be, then, just like *that*, we shift, scraping against each other like rigid plates fighting for space; we subduct, slide, and separate with seismic force, leaving messy rifts. It's life on a fault line, it's hell on the libido, and it's taking its toll.

Coming back from my visit to Seattle lands me in a funk. I miss my Seattle friends; I miss having lots of help. I miss the easy way JB and I got along for the rest of those hot Spokane days (and nights . . .). I'm starting to realize that I'm pretty isolated. Lonely, I spend the days trolling parks and grocery store aisles like a mother-vulture, waiting for opportunities to swoop down and pick up information and context for this new life. I join a baby-friendly aerobics class but find the moms aren't nearly so friendly. They're competitive and cliquey, laughing at inside jokes, complaining about their bodies, making excuses for their babies' fussiness. "He's out of sorts today," says one, but I get a sense from the fatigue in her voice and the knowing looks exchanged by the others that he's often out of sorts, that tomorrow he'll be just as out of sorts. Only one of the mothers bothers introducing herself to me. Our one-way conversation consists of her telling me how skinny I am, how I don't need to work out, how she used to look like me, once, before she had kids. It's true that I'm losing weight fast. I'm skinnier than I've been in years, having lost my baby weight and beyond. But it's not a healthy, fit kind of thin; it's a too-tired-to-eat, running-myself-ragged thin.

"You look tired," my mom says, on one of our rare afternoon spoiling outings, and for a minute I think she looks wistful. I know she's proud of me as a mother. I know she can tell that in many ways, I'm happier than I've been in a long time, and I know she loves my daughter endlessly. But sometimes, knowing her own choices in life, I can't help but think she wanted more for me.

I look tired because I am. I'm pale and waiflike, with dark circles under my eyes. By noon every day I'm exhausted, despite the fact that my one-year-old baby sleeps ten hours a night and naps regularly. I chalk it up to my domestic overdrive and unending maternal vigilance, my new second nature, but the thought lingers in me that something more is going on, something physical.

"Maybe you're pregnant," someone in my moms' group says, smiling evilly. I force a smile back, but cringe inside. It's not impossible, though it is unlikely. Ironically, after employing extremely passive and, dare I say, idiotic birth control methods for the first half of my sexual life, I am now in a situation where it would be entirely appropriate to get pregnant—and I've become a birth-control fascist. As we're snuggled in bed, my husband's foot accidentally grazes mine—and I am prepared. "No cover, no lover," I state, pulling the sheet to cover any skin I may have irresponsibly exposed. Bewildered, he takes the time to remind me that our daughter is sleeping between us, that he has to wake up painfully early, and that, despite my overwhelming charm, he is simply not in the mood. "Still," I say, scooting to safety on my side of the bed, "you can never be too safe."

We have been safe—mostly—but accidents do happen. Pregnancies, planned and unplanned, are popping up around me like magic mushrooms: my sister-in-law, two women in my moms' group, a former coworker. Although I'm still nursing and haven't even gotten my period yet, pregnancy paranoia is always there on my mind, it's yet another thing to worry about, yet another player in the "Bye-bye, libido" game. It's also the source of another rift between me and my husband. Birth control is our second favorite fight now, right on the heels of our infamous "Who does more work?" argument—and they're not unrelated. Birth control is another responsibility that defaults to me lately. I'm the one who always has to think of it and enforce it, and I'm the one, quite frankly, stuck doing all the work if we get pregnant. If my husband had his druthers, he'd never wear a condom. "It's like wearing a shower curtain," he complains. He's always trying to sneak around my rules and get in for free without one. "I'll pull out," he promises, going strong, but I've seen the statistics (and bouncing baby boys) that come from that tactic. Not to mention that it leaves me feeling like a hall monitor: *Are you* still *in there? Shouldn't you be somewhere else right now, young man?* It's hardly a way to get lost in the moment. Over the years we've tried just about every brand of condom; we've tried lubricated, nonlubricated, ribbed, and special "for her" condoms. We've tried the Maxx large size to give him more room (go me!). We've even tried flavored. But according to him, they're all dulling, they all bring the act down a notch.

Of course, he had pitch-perfect condom use as a young man; it was one of his endearing qualities to me. He was responsible, he never got anyone pregnant, he didn't spread or contract anything uncivilized. He credits his adoptive dad's sex talk for his good record, three simple words about the birds and bees: "Use a condom." I credit the fact that he grew up with a mother who had kids so young; he didn't want to make the same mistake. He always wanted to do better with his own kids, to be able to give them everything that he'd missed. For some reason, though, his acceptance of condoms seems to have gone the way of open relationships and pajama pants.

But as much as he complains, he knows better than to ask me to go back on the pill. *The Libido Torpedo,* he calls it, remembering past times I've tried it. It's true—a little like the baldness-curing medicine that makes men impotent (or is it the other way around?), the pill let me have worry-free sex whenever I wanted it . . . except I never, ever wanted it. For a long time I thought it was just in my head, until I finally asked my doctor, who confessed that lack of desire for sex was a potential side effect; she said it had something to do with the way the pill suppresses the body's natural level of hormones. She tried to convince me to try a different brand, or use something else, but I was over it. I'd done my time on that end of things. And now, it's his turn—and all things considered, he's getting the easy end of the deal. *Oh,*

Oh, poor baby, does a condom feel like a shower curtain?

TRY CHILDBIRTH, BUDDY.

poor baby, does it feel like a shower curtain? Try childbirth, buddy. Try morning sickness and raw, bleeding nipples for a while. He knows damn well I'm not ready to go through another pregnancy or have another baby, and he says he's not ready, either. But then every time we have sex, I'm the one stuck enforcing the rules. I don't think he whines or cajoles or "forgets" on purpose—I think he just gets caught up in the moment and assumes I am too. But I'm not. I'm on call, on duty. And totally turned off by it. This is what it tells me: *This is all on you. This is your deal, not mine.*

It is Communication Breakdown 101. He wants to make me feel good, to pleasure me, to be as close as he can to me without latex getting in the way. He's trying to say *I love you, be close to me.* But I don't hear that at all; what I hear is that he doesn't seem to have any idea what's important to me these days, that he has no idea how overwhelmed with responsibilities I already am. I'm hearing that he doesn't really care about anything except spreading his seed. Because if he did care, he wouldn't even come near me without a condom already on and the dishes done.

The fights we had before the baby were fiery and passionate, about things that mattered to us: We argued over public-school busing practices, we fought when he thought I was dismissing his outrage that his world literature class didn't include any authors of color, and we fought like crazy if jealousy came into the picture. Once, I sucker-punched him because I thought he was flirting with someone else. Another time he railed at me for days about the way I let a "gay" friend (not really so gay, and not such a friend, it turned out) put his hands on my hips. Maybe it wasn't always healthy, but it was always heated, and it *always* resulted in earthshaking make-up sex. The morning after one of these fights, I woke up to find a love note on my pillow. JB had taped Polaroids of us in the act onto lined yellow paper and drawn arrows pointing to each of us. "*He* loves *her* so much he gets the shakes," was all it said, and that said it all.

Now, we're on shakier ground. Now, we're tense and uptight, always waiting for the Big One. Parenting on a fault line is volatile. Emotions and hormones run high and wild, sleep is scarce, and time is at a premium, it is never on our side. We float through the weeks in a blurry baby haze. We fight about dishes, and who cleans the house, and sex. We fight about who did what, and whose turn it is, and how to do it right. "You just don't understand," I snap at him, trying to explain what it's like

What I'm really trying to say is: Hold me. Tell me I'm doing a good job. Tell me I'm **NOT IN THIS ALONE.**

to be on call all the time. What I'm really trying to say is: *Hold me. Tell me I'm doing a good job. Tell me I'm not in this alone.* What I really want is to feel close to him again, to get back to where we were, but I'm not very good at asking for help. I'm not very good at asking for what I need.

"Okay," he says, playing his card, doing his part to keep the fight going. "Let's switch. It's my turn to stay home with the baby. You go back to work." That's his A-bomb, his nuclear answer; he knows I won't call his bluff. I hiss and pour myself a glass of wine.

Really, I think we're fighting about something bigger than the workload, something harder to put a finger on. I think we're fighting because these days we don't have enough time for ourselves, much less each other. Panicked about what we've given up, we're being selfish and defensive, fighting for the ugly scraps of What Was. I used to wake up in the morning and think, *What would make my husband happy today? What can I do for this man I love? How can I help him?* Now, I wake up first—and resent it. Now I have a running list of ways he's falling behind and not pulling his weight. My husband, who used to wake me up with predawn kisses on my back, call me his "queen," and buy me flowers for no reason, now calls me "Mommy" and skips the flowers to buy Elmo balloons for our daughter. He knows better than to try to touch me; he knows my daughter will shriek in delight at Elmo, where I will just plain shriek about anything.

"You're tracking mud," I grunt as soon as my husband gets home from work. I'm not passive-aggressive about it. I'm aggressive-aggressive. My frustration about my long list of domestic tasks is turning into resentment. I live with two messy people who undo the only things I have accomplished all day. I do them again, bitter. I hate the dishwasher, hate the laundry, hate playing pat-a-cake. I clean the floors, and our two dogs leave muddy paw prints all over them. I put toys away, and my daughter gleefully ransacks them. I shop for food, and my husband eats it all in one late-night binge.

I grew up with the idea that parenting and housework were a fifty-fifty kind of thing, that mothers and fathers were exact equal partners. I thought I would happily stay home with our daughter, maybe even see my husband off to work with lunch and kisses. And then after work, he and I would share household duties, dividing perfectly the after-dinner hours and weekends. We'd trade off waking up at night. He'd stay with the baby while I went out partying with my friends, and vice versa. The vision I had was so empowering, so *fair*, so much better than the housewifery of old. I *chose* this life for myself, in part by choosing to marry such a smart, sensitive, progressive man. A man who has taken more women's studies classes than I have. A man whose youthful band, Sammitch, had a crowd-pleasin' favorite called "Menses Man." (*menses man got a mission/menses man got a cause/menses man got a fascination for menopause/he's got uterus envy/thinks childbearin's swell/likes his penis fine but he wants somethin' else as well. . . .*) My husband is the one who will teach our daughter the history of feminism. He is the one who will take her to see the WNBA. And he is also the one who has no idea where the Tupperware goes. We may have come "a long way, baby" in the world outside the home and the family, but within it, we still have a long way to go. Although back in school I repeatedly failed algebra, I am convinced there is an equation to explain the relationship between this gap and my lost libido. Variables of time and titillation, work and wetness, romance and resentment, all come into play. It's about dirt and depletion, nursing and nookie, hormones and heat, fucking and fucking up.

"Oh, I see the Bitching Hour has begun."

This is my progressive husband being not so sensitive, not so smart. I have a deep, grumbling urge to bite his face. But part of me knows he's right. All this hyper housewifing is making me a little, er, desperate. By the time he gets home from work at seven, I am a wild-eyed she-monster. I flinch when he takes the baby from me, then follow the two of them around, pouncing on each fuss, each cry, each thing he is doing wrong. When I point out the mildew clouds growing in the shower, my husband asks if I can make him a chore chart. This is his liberated "Menses Man" response? *A chore chart?* What am I, his fucking stepmother? I don't doubt (well, okay, maybe I do a little) that he would complete any assigned chores on a chore chart, but the last thing I want to be is the chore-chart maker. I'm not the boss of him. I'm tired of being the default grownup, the default parent.

Of course, I'm not the only one with a running list of frustrations; he's keeping track, too. Backed into a childish time-out-like corner, my husband fights back, lashing out with a checklist of his own—how many times we've had sex in the past week, the past month, the past year. Because I have the power to veto it, sex is another thing that defaults to me these days, and the fact that we aren't having enough of it is all about me and my issues. *My* issues. Here are some of *my* issues: In the past year since having a baby I have withheld sex because I was angry. I have pretended to be asleep. I have wondered when it would be over so I could check my email or clean the house. I have muttered under my breath, "Grow the fuck up." My issues are like the rowdy bad kid of the family, always in the hot spot, always pushing everyone else into the background and getting the most attention—even if it's the bad kind.

If I weren't so tired and caught up in my own frustrations and issues, I might be able to see some of my husband's. I might see a man who is tired of being rejected, tired of fighting, and tired of getting in trouble like a little boy for doing everything the wrong way. I might notice the unseen work he does, too: the comp time he's accrued working late nights and through lunches; the extra classes he takes to make sure he's on top of things, to make sure he's providing for us the best he can.

"Why don't you just go take a break or something?" my husband says, tired of being harped on. It's another communication breakdown. What he's really trying to say is: *Where did you go, wife? Where's the fun in this?* He's saying, *Hey, don't leave me and go to the bird people. Come back, come back and be with me like we used to be*. But I can't hear it over the din of my building resentment. All I hear is the practiced paternalistic voice I know he employs when he wants to press my bitchy buttons.

He cements things by picking up the baby and pushing away the dinner I made, without having so much as a bite. The hot, delicious, dish-dirtying dinner—not just another one-pot wonder—that I took more than an hour to make; the dinner he didn't ask for, but that I made for him anyway, *just because*; the dinner I'd already shoved down in gulping bites while I played with my daughter, too hungry from not eating all day to wait for him to get home from work. A bubbling, out-of-control rage starts up in me. I'm not sure where this one's coming from—I want to blame it on hormones, but a year into things I'm hardly postpartum. *Why don't you go fuck yourself?* I think. I want to throw his plate of food against the wall, scream and yell, and then force the cold broccoli side dish down his throat. But instead I shut down, lock up, and blink back angry tears. A fight is not on the schedule for tonight; it's not part of the environment I've carefully constructed to hold everything together, to make it through the day. How did I get to this point? When *did* I become so rigid? Why *don't* I take a break?

Here's the thing. Co-parenting, that ridiculously named concept decreeing that mothers and fathers have an equal workload, is a myth. Don't get me wrong: It's a lovely, righteous ideal. I want it to be real as much as I once wanted the Land of Narnia to be. But as far as I can tell, my wardrobe is still just a wardrobe, and when it comes to the baby I still end up doing the lion's share. I guess should have listened a little better to my *Free to Be . . . You and Me* album. Because now, replaying the song "Parents Are People," dancing around the house with my tiny partner, I'm hit by a line I never really heard before. Right after the part about mommies being anything they want to be, there is another that says daddies can be anything they want to be also, except, of course, mommies. And there's the rub. Because that's exactly what our daughter wants most days, and nights, and everything in between: her mommy. To my daughter, my husband is a mildly amusing character with a serious equipment deficiency. She's even forgiving of that, at times taking a bottle, flirting with him from my arms, or squealing as he throws her up in the air. But she can't get past his one true fault: He's just not me.

I know I should take a break. I know could. At almost a year, our daughter can handle being upset, and he is her dad, after all. He's entirely capable of handling her if I'd just let him. But the truth is, I don't want to. Not because she'll cry, or won't eat well, or will be fussy and sour the next day, and not because sometimes it's more work to leave her than it's worth. It's something bigger. It's a drive I have to be with her; it's the addictive drug of maternal attachment; it's the way, workload be damned, it just feels right. While I was pregnant, I had fantasies of my mom coming over and holding the baby while I caught up on sleep or snuggled with JB. Days after the actual birth, my mom came by to do just that; she sat in the living room holding the baby while I tossed and turned in bed, exhausted but unable to sleep. I wasn't worried about the baby; I knew she was fine. But I was incomplete without her. Finally my mom went back to work, I lay back down with my daughter nestled on my chest, and within minutes we were both sound asleep.

From the other room I listen as my husband and daughter make faces at each other and laugh, as he changes her diaper, and as she gets more and more fussy. I listen as he tries to figure out what I already know: She's tired, she's teething, she wants to nurse. It's strange and unnerving for him, too, this uneven aspect of parenting. It's not the way either one of us thought it would be, and it messes with his confidence and ego. He's used to being good at everything. He's used to having all women love him.

"I think the baby needs you," my husband finally admits, and brings me my tired, teary-eyed girl. *Of course she does,* I think, and despite myself I get a boost. I'm filled with a dangerous kind of satisfaction—the idea that I can give my daughter something that no one else can, that she needs me more than anything or anyone else in the world, and that I don't need anything or anyone else than her. It also gives me the illusion of being in control. With so much chaos in our lives, JB and I are each trying to find comfort in control, wherever we can. Life on the edge of the rocky, volatile fault of our marriage is a cliffhanger; I'm holding on by my fingernails, digging into whatever I can of our old life. I'm trying to somehow bitch things back to normal, to wicked-witch my way back to the ease and closeness we had before. I look for comfort in strict schedules, clean floors, and mildew-free showers. My husband looks for it in job security, in perfecting his skills, in the inanimate and predictable comfort of computer code that makes a lot more sense to him than I do these days.

Sex as communication has long since broken down for us. Like with the tasty hot dinner thing, I assume my husband wants sex, or needs it. But the truth is, he'd much rather order a pizza than see me stress out over a hot stove. He'd much rather pass on sex altogether than participate in what he has so sensitively dubbed "corpse sex." But I don't know this yet. Panicked about our lack of connection, about the way he pulls away from me, the way the baby has come between us, I've made the mistake of assuming he would prefer pity sex to none at all. I'm becoming very guylike about the whole act. I'm over foreplay; I find it an excruciating waste of time. I want sex to be quick and efficient, not all touchy-feely. I'm goal-oriented and geared toward him: The faster we get there, the better. I want him to get in, get some, and get out. Sometimes, this businesslike approach really works for me; sometimes it even turns me on. But most times it's like a dirty payoff—he gets his sex and I get to feel dutiful, but really it's hurting us both. Rather than getting connection out of the deal, we're getting bitter. We're having—and I can't believe I'm saying this—*bad sex.*

Let me explain. *Bad sex* is not in our vocabulary. Bad sex is for proms and one-night stands with guys in the Canadian navy (as I can attest). Bad sex is, like, so *totally* 1992. It's just not us. We're the anti–bad sex. Even when I broke my femur (oh yes, ouch) showing off on the stupid, hellbound motorcycle JB bought right after meeting me (proof he really was trying to destroy his life), within two weeks—of major surgery, mind you—we were fooling around again. Even when I couldn't, wouldn't, or didn't dare move my leg, we had good sex. Thanks to some excellent meds I don't remember *how* it was good, I don't remember *what* about it was so good, but I do remember *why* it was good. It was good because we were in love with each other, crutches and gauze and all. It was good because we were on the road to becoming *us*; unstoppable, unflappable, undeniably us. And it was hot. We knew it; we didn't have to talk about it or go over the details.

LET ME EXPLAIN.

Bad sex is not in our vocabulary. Bad sex is for proms and one-night stands.

Though these days we have no problem talking about our mismatched sex drives ("You *never* want sex!" "Yeah? Well, you *always* want sex!"), we still don't talk about the physical details of sex very much at all. We want it to be intuitive, immediate, automatic. We want to be as connected sexually as we were then, without actually verbally connecting about it.

In an attempt to get out of our bitch and bitchee roles, we've decided to institute "date night," something all the magazine articles suggest but something I've been against—probably because I know who is going to be stuck with all the planning and arranging. My mom has agreed to watch the baby every Friday, but my daughter, at a year old, is in full separation-anxiety mode, and the feeling is mutual. I hate leaving her. Not because I'm worried that my mom can't handle the baby (she's got backup: ice cream) or that the baby can't handle being away from me, but because it's just so much easier *not* to leave her. Out there—in the big, scary world—anything could happen to me. And while I do worry about my daughter, the truth is, I'm feeling vulnerable and exposed, too. "Out there"—in the world without our daughter—there's no one to interrupt us or steal the show; there's no excuse to stop fighting, or to not have sex, or to watch junky TV and go to bed early. Out there, it's just us. Which is exactly why we need to go.

For tonight's date, we are celebrating Valentine's Day a week early, our second Valentine's Day since the baby was born. Despite a habit of notoriously forgetting anniversaries, JB has always come through on Valentine's Day; there are always at least flowers, or a homemade card, or a fancy dinner. It was on a Valentine's Day that he first told me he was ready to live together, so many years ago, leaving a tiny gold-plated Monopoly house on my pillow before leaving for work. Our first Valentine's Day with the baby came just two days after she was born; that, too, was beautiful and poignant, but not exactly romantic. At the time I was overcome with love and milk and meaning, awed by my husband (for his steady genes, and for co-creating clearly the most amazing human being that had ever come into existence), and shocked that with all the excitement he'd managed to plan ahead, setting a silver box on my lap in the hospital bed. I remember feeling deliriously guilty for a minute that I had nothing for him—no chocolate, no champagne, no red teddy. At least I could have made him a card.

In the box on that Valentine's Day were three silver bracelets, nesting in soft white lining. I felt like Goldilocks as I fingered each one: the big heavy one with FATHER engraved on it, the teeny tiny one engraved with our daughter's name, and there, for me, the perfect, medium-sized one, the just-right one, engraved with my my new role: MOTHER.

At the time, I didn't get the symbolism. I couldn't see the implicit deal that was going down; neither of us could. How could we know the real weight of that word around my wrist? Or the way it was already etched in my heart? How could we know how easy it was going to be to trade romantic love in for mother-love? Or how hard it would be to mesh the two?

This Valentine's Day I had hoped to be a little more

prepared. I considered some options: Maybe I would greet him at the door in lingerie, or pick up a new sex toy, or feed him oysters naked. But those things would take so much planning and shopping and, well, work. And my daughter seems to have other plans—like spiking a fever, throwing up, and projectile pooping. There's nothing quite like a sick baby to remind everyone who the primary parent is. When my daughter is sick she wants nothing but me; she wants to nurse literally nonstop. She cries if I leave the room to use the toilet. I had a blankie *and* a binky when I was a baby, but my daughter has no such pre-vices. She has me. I am her security blanket, I'm her lovey.

Never was that primary caregiving role more clear to me than the night I woke up with a horrible burning, stinging urge to pee when my daughter was just three months old. I sat on the toilet for hours, uncontrollably peeing blood, until finally the on-call doctor phoned me back and told me I probably had a urinary tract infection. With nothing to do but wait for a morning appointment (or wait for hours in the emergency room, without the comfort of my own toilet right there), and with no one else capable of nursing my daughter (who was refusing bottles then), I shoved a couple of her tiny diapers in my underwear and lay in bed, peeing and nursing her and crying. My husband put his arm around me and asked if there was anything he could do, but of course there wasn't. And within minutes he was asleep again, and I was awake: burning, incontinent, and in pain, listening to him snore and hating him for it.

Although my daughter gets better just in time for our big date, I'm an exhausted wreck. So much for sexy plans—getting dressed and staying awake is about all I can offer. Determined not to ruin things, though, and fairly sure my husband hasn't planned anything beyond the roses he sent from work this morning, I make a quick call to the hot tub place where we have an unused gift certificate, a much-belated wedding present from a family friend. Cupid smiles: I book the last available tub for the night.

Hot tubs, like motel rooms, have always been good to us. There's something about them—the heat, the water, the outright nakedness of the whole thing—that just really works. They remind us of hot, sex-filled days spent vacationing in the sun. The first vacation we ever took together we drove east out of the Bay Area until we hit scorching heat, pulling into a divey motel in Chico. We spent a long weekend lounging in the heat by the deserted pool and having sex on the

Hot tubs, like motel rooms,
HAVE ALWAYS BEEN GOOD TO US.

cool white sheets in our room. Later, on that trip to Acapulco, we did the same, spending nearly all day nearly naked next to each other in the pool, then heading to our room where our bodies emanated heat and lust and electricity on the cool kitchenette floor. We started going to spas as a way to find privacy from a flat full of roommates, and we kept going because the nice ones are like mini-vacations: heat, crisp cool sheets, and temporary shelter from the real world.

We get to the spa half an hour early, so we jet across the street to an old-timers' bar and each order a shot. When the bartender asks what we're up to, we giggle, then spontaneously lie and tell him we're headed to a movie, the lie suddenly upping the naughtiness factor. Because we both know what *hot tub* really means, by the time we're actually in the tub it's hard to think about anything else; the pressure to have sex is right up there with the pressure to go out on New Year's Eve. I slink to the other side of the tub, hiding my body under the water and wishing for a minute I was by myself so I could really relax and enjoy this. Fortunately the heat and the shots (don't try this at home) loosen us up, and we start talking—about past Valentine's Days, about other hot tub experiences, about something funny that happened at work—and then, surprisingly, he mentions he's brought some new lambskin condoms he'd like to try.

Frankly, I'm shocked—but in a good way. Not because the idea of animal intestine inside me is kind of weird—which it is—but because I can't believe his initiative in the matter. So, wow. Here he is, with a box of condoms in his pocket, ready to use. And here we are, two adults in a private little open-air island. Maybe he does care—maybe sometimes he really does get me. I scoot a little closer to him. Our feet touch, our legs touch, and then things start to heat up pretty fast. Lightheaded, I sit on the edge of the tub while he massages my feet. I lay back on the cool tiles and look up at the stars. "I miss you," my husband says as he kisses my ankles and moves slowly, generously, up. "I hate the way we fight."

I miss me, too. I hate the bitchy, frenzied person I've become. I hate the way I'm greedy for control, the way I can't let go, the way I care too much about dirt and chores and other things I swore I'd never fight over. It occurs to me that motherhood and sex—at least, good sex—really aren't that compatible. Good sex is all about letting go, getting lost in the moment, in sensation, in another person. But being a good mother is about holding on—holding things together, holding out for the best life you can give your child. No wonder scrapbooking is so popular with the at-home set. It's what we're trained to do: keep it all together, keep it all safe, keep from losing what matters most to us.

I'm pulled from that line of thought by my sudden sense of urgency. With only twenty minutes left on our room, I'm wet, my thighs are quivering, and I'm shaking with hunger. I pull him close to me; I feel his heat as he drips all over me, sliding, slipping, dripping. I'm ready to make the earth move again, to spin and get caught up in the moment, *magnitude ten.* With heat and blood pounding through me, I'm ready to explode. I'm ready, for right now at least, to start letting go.

BECOMING MINE

CHAPTER 4

When you feel the warm sun

on your face again

you will fly

spread your wings

butterfly

—LISA LOEB, "BUTTERFLY"

there is another equation I can't quite get a handle on these days. It has something to do with good sex and connection, and bad sex and disconnection. It's a logic puzzle, of sorts, or maybe just a classic vicious circle. Each time we have bad sex, we pull away from each other a little. Each time we pull away from each other a little, I get hungrier for connection and retreat more into my daughter, getting my intimacy fix from her. The more I retreat into my daughter, the more JB gets left behind, and the more distance stretches between us. The more distance that stretches between us, the less I want to have sex with him; the less I feel like having sex, the more bad sex we have, the more we pull away from each other again, and so on. The solution seems simple on paper: Stop pulling away from each other. Connect. Have bad sex less. Have good sex more.

The wildcard in all of this, though, is my maternal consumption, the overwhelming connection I'm already getting from mother-love. Since I have 24/7 access to intimacy, I'm not jonesing for it in the same way my husband is. Matters are made worse by the fact that sex was once JB's surefire way of reaching out to me, of asking for that intimacy. I know this about him; it's part of what makes saying "no" so hard, and it's why I keep having sex when I really don't want it.

"Well, she's asleep," I say. "We better do this thing." This is my now-classic all-charm approach. Motive (he wants it) and opportunity (the baby's in the other room) have converged, and I just can't pass it up. JB is clearly not impressed with my come-on, but at this point, he'll take what he can get. I start stripping off layers of oversized flannel pajamas and climb under the covers with him. "Get on top of me," I order him; the missionary position has become the mercenary position. *Get in. Get the job done. Get out.* When he tries to kiss my chest I have an urge to shout "No!" and shove him off me, but soon he's moved on. He works his way inside me and I gasp because it hurts; I'm dry still from nursing hormones, and as usual, I'm not really turned on. Mistaking my gasp for the kind of gasps he used to get out of me pre-baby, my husband finds new energy, flipping me on top of him where he can watch me, where he knows I usually like to be. He's so into it that I play along, trying to let go and get into it. Soon, though, I'm self-conscious about the way my breasts are flapping like music clackers, the pressure of the quick motion making them feel full and sore. I've just about worked up the courage to admit I need to stop, I need a break, when I'm saved by the bell: A loud shriek from our baby in the other room makes us both stop. She screams again, and this time my milk lets down in response, leaking all over my husband's chest. I know in certain circles people pay money to see that kind of thing, but I'm not one of them. We look at each other and laugh as I roll off him, pretending to be bummed.

If I could speak honestly to JB, I would tell him that my daughter's cries had hit me in the same place that things like chocolate and memories of good lazy sex do: in my pleasure center, my happy spot. I would tell him how I was really grateful for the interruption, grateful to sit on the couch with her hot skin on mine and nurse her back to the perfect, quiet sleep she still wears like a newborn.

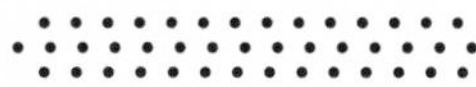

At just a little over a year old, my daughter makes her first real joke; she grabs my boob in her chubby paws, grins hugely, and announces, "Mine!" I might have found this funny and cute if she (and therefore, I) hadn't been up all night, leisurely grazing on breastmilk—or if I hadn't just spent an hour of precious naptime arguing with my sad and neglected husband about our sex life (or lack thereof). Just minutes before, I'd yelled, *"Get the [*bleep*] away from me!"* at my sad and neglected dog after she laid her head on my lap for a long-overdue petting session; I'm clearly not up for humor.

She grabs my boob in her chubby paws, grins hugely, and announces, "MINE!"

The problem is, my daughter's first devil-inspired try at humor got it right. Contrary to what my husband might hope for, my breasts do still belong to her. And that's just the beginning. My heart, my attention, my total devotion—they all still also belong to her. It's her scent I inhale at night. It's her skin I polish with kisses. It's her body I know better than my husband's now, better than mine. I have no biological rhythm or cycle of my own anymore, a clear reminder that being a mother is the priority here—being a woman, not so much. Being a lover, even less.

So, a couple months later, despite the telltale mood swings and cramps I've had all week, my period comes as a total surprise to me; I'm unprepared and nearly as upset about it as Sissy Spacek was in *Carrie*. Surely I would get a longer reprieve. After all, my tank of a toddler, at fifteen months, is a champion breastfeeder; she's dedicated and professional about it. After a rough start latching on in the early weeks, she quickly honed her skills and even now seems to have no interest in giving it up. I, too, have no interest in encouraging her to stop; I'm as hooked as she is. I can count on breastfeeding to always bring her back to me, to squeeze a good long snuggle in between activities, and to balance the times she bites me or hits me in the face, accidentally-on-purpose. It's harder and harder to be discreet about it, though, as she gets more mobile and more verbal. "Boo-bee, Mama," she says with immodest clarity, regardless of where we are.

She treats my breast like a bottle, trying to take it with her as she toddles off, giving up only when she's stretched my nipple as far as it will go, then letting go with an expert flourish as it snaps back. I'm surprised by my own lack of modesty; I have no problem whipping my breast out willy-nilly. I'm sure it has something to do with living in Berkeley, one of the few places in the country where new mothers are shamed more for bottle-feeding than anything else; here, people wear Boobs not Bombs T-shirts, and in 2002 we beat the *Guinness Book of World*

Records for most moms breastfeeding at one time. It's more than just that, though, because I'm usually the kind of person who would rather eat runny eggs than cause a fuss by sending them back. For some reason, when it comes to my daughter I have no problem speaking up or breaking with social rules. Her needs come first—before my anxiety, before others' discomfort, before society's hang-ups. It's a surprising bonus; for my daughter I have the voice I've always lacked, even if I don't always know how to use it yet.

"You can't live through your kids," the facilitator of my mothers' group says that Thursday at our regular meeting. She's talking about the competitive nature of motherhood—how so many of us judge and are judged, how we push our kids to make ourselves feel better and help us fill the gaps in our own lives. One mother is upset because her fourteen-month-old has no real vocabulary yet; she's worried he'll fall behind, or do poorly in school, or have trouble making friends. Suddenly I find myself joining the judgmental ranks. *Give the kid a break,* I think. *He's a baby, for Christ's sake.* But that's easy for me to say. My daughter is not only insanely cute (no, really, she is; I've been randomly handed more than one modeling agent's card. It's genetic—old ladies walking down the street used to hand my mother-in-law money just because JB was such a beautiful baby); she's also verbally precocious. "Big. Knife. Mama," she told me that morning, eyes wide in awe as she stood on tippy-toe to pull a butcher knife the size of her forearm off the counter. "Biiiig." But of course, who's judging now, right? What kind of mom leaves a butcher knife out where a curious toddler can grab it?

For me the real problem is that I'm not used to my daughter's new mobility, or her growing independence. I can't believe the things she can suddenly do. I can't believe there are times I reach for her now and she pulls away.

When it's my turn to talk in the group I don't talk about this, though; I complain about getting my period, about having cramps and being even more tired, and about having yet another diaper-type mess to deal with. The facilitator reminds me of the bright side; she tells me my libido should start making a comeback, and that I'm starting to get my body back, my life back. *What body?* I think. *What did it ever really do for me before childbirth?* I quit running track and playing soccer when I discovered boys. *What life?* Most of my pre-baby life seems suddenly insignificant, as does my sex drive. For me, mother-love is the Big Bang; before it, I'm certain, I

For me, mother-love is **THE BIG BANG;** *before it, I was nothing but matterless empty space.*

was nothing but matterless empty space. Mother love exploded into me like pure energy, burrowing into every part, homing in on my dark, empty places and filling them with light and brilliance. It took over, pushing out, dwarfing everything else I used to be, everything else I used to think mattered—including, but of course not limited to, sex.

The next day is Friday—date night again. A wonderful concept, in theory, but so far left mostly to theory. Tonight is no exception. I call my husband at work to cancel; *I'm bloated, I'm too tired, the baby's too tired, it's never going to work, I have nothing to wear.* My husband says, "Okay," but I can hear the disappointment in his voice. I can also hear his coworkers in the background, inviting him to hit happy hour with them. He asks me to hold on, and I hear a woman's laugh, teasing him (or is that flirting?) about some work-related thing—something he really understands, something other than chore-related lectures and baby minutiae, something about life in the real world, something that matters to him.

Jealousy and insecurity get the better of me. "I'll meet you at seven," I say, and hang up.

When I get to my mom's house, she and her fiancé are just sitting down for dinner. I'm happy to see him, not just because two sets of hands are always better than one when it comes to a fussy baby, but because I'm so happy about their engagement;

he's a catch. He's sweet, sane, doting, and determined: a perfect balance to my mom's charming but complicated intensity. They're content to stay engaged, and have no plans to seal the deal. He has muscular dystrophy, and I think the uncertainty of his future helped her get over her fear of commitment: She can promise him forever, because it's not clear what that means.

For as long as I can remember my mom has had this fear about not being able to hold on to herself when she's with other people. She gives and gives so much, so intensely, that she loses her footing, she slips under, making her feel so lost and smothered and panicked that she sees no other choice than to leave and find herself again. That's partly what happened with her and my dad. It's also, I think, what happened with her as a young mother. I'm determined not to do the same thing—so determined, in fact, that I'm heading toward the same place. I'm holding on to my daughter so tight, it's forcing leaks into other parts of my life. Maybe that's one reason why it's so hard for me to relax and let go and really enjoy sex: I'm afraid if I let go, the dam will break. Maybe I'm afraid to let go of anything because I'll start to lose it all.

While my daughter gets settled in at my mom's, I panic and run upstairs to quickly scribble my last will and testament, leaving explicit directions for the care of our daughter should my husband and I die in a freak car accident. I hide the paper deep in the diaper bag and hope my mom doesn't find it unless, knock on wood, she really needs to. Although I was convinced my newborn daughter would die in the short car ride from hospital to home (I still can't believe they let us leave with her; surely they could tell we had no idea what we were doing), I'm now beginning to see the possibility that she just might survive her babyhood. Instead of relishing that and relaxing, in classic-me style I simply funnel my anxieties into a whole new arena: my own tragic demise. Now that I can actually imagine that my daughter might end up okay (pending no more incidents involving "big knives," at least), I'm pretty sure that *I* won't; I'm haunted by the thought of accidentally abandoning her.

Car accidents are just one of the many possible scenarios I entertain; lately, I find myself favoring "The Big C," cancer. I'm pretty confident I have a brain tumor, one that's slowly growing until one day I just won't wake up. A morbid film loops in my head: Some morning, well after my husband leaves for work, my daughter will cry and reach to wake me up as usual. She'll put her fingers in my mouth, and give me fat open kisses on my cheek. But I'll be dead, unable to comfort her as she cries and tries to nurse. Finally, she'll fall asleep until my husband gets home, devastated to find us.

I haven't told my husband about my fears. I feel silly when I say them out loud, and I don't want to worry him. He's doing such a good job of being the sane one, putting up with my crankiness and mood swings, working long hours at the office and taking cute forays into father-appropriate hobbies like woodworking (he almost lost a finger) and auto repair (our car is still not the same). Actually, I've noticed, he's taking up just about anything that'll take his mind off the connection he hasn't been getting from me.

Nowadays I lie to him not only about not wanting sex, but about how tired and out of control I feel inside. I hide that from everyone—from him, from my mom, from my friends in my moms' group, and especially from my daughter. No matter how exhausted I am, I put on a smile for her. I do what I do best: I set my own needs aside, quiet my own voice, and hide everything under a cloak of perfection. I wish I could remember how to talk to my husband about real things—how to give to him better, how to tell him what I need. But lately we're just ghosts to each other, passing in the hall and bathroom and clinking our chains. I can barely see him; I barely have the energy to make out the silent signals he's trying to give me, the ones I used to be able to read like fireworks.

By the time I get out of my mom's, I'm already late meeting JB. I feel self-conscious as I walk into the dark, downtown Oakland hipster bar. I blink while my eyes adjust to the darkness; it's like visiting a nocturnal house at the zoo. I feel out of place, out of my element, vulnerable. I'm a daylight person now.

I spent most of today outside in the bright California sun, trying to walk off my cramps, knee-high in weeds and wildflowers at the Berkeley Marina. Thankfully my daughter was a good sport in her backpack, shrieking in delight at the monarchs circling us. "Butterfly," I'd say and point, and she'd clap and laugh and wrap her arms around my neck, where I could kiss the dimples on her chubby hands.

I finally spot JB sitting with friends from work, and wish I had dressed up more. This is the after-work crowd. They're dressed for success; I'm dressed for survival. They wear cute suits and nice shoes, and probably remember deodorant. My husband waves and walks over to meet me, smiling. He moves to kiss my cheek, but I instinctively turn away and focus instead on the plastic butterfly someone has taped to the cash register. "Butterfly," I say and point it out to no one in particular.

When we get home our daughter is asleep in her carseat, so we sit in front of the house listening to music on the radio. We laugh about the night he proposed, remembering the dumb, cheesy song that was playing on the only station we got in that car—a catchy pop song we hated but didn't turn off either. We remember the sound of the rain on the corrugated plastic roof of the carport, and I mention how after four years of being together I was convinced he would never get around to asking me to marry him. We reminisce about another trip we took to Reno, to visit his brother. We stayed at Circus Circus and walked around looking at rings in pawnshop windows. I thought for sure he was going to surprise me by popping the question during that trip—he was being extra sweet—and it wasn't until we were about an hour's drive outside of San Francisco that I finally couldn't stand it anymore. "So, you're really not going to ask me to marry you?" I asked, disappointed, and he almost choked on his Big Gulp.

Still laughing, we agree we should have just gotten married that first night we met. I lean on his shoulder, then lean in closer and we kiss; it's nice. I know we won't end up in the backseat, because it's already taken up by a sacked-out lump of baby. We kiss again, and I realize how much I've missed just making out. After getting married, we usually skipped that step and went straight for the hard stuff. I flash back to the first time I made out with a boy: I was twelve. My girlfriends and I had snuck out and met up with a kid from school. Somehow, he and I ended up together; it was gross and thrilling at the same time. *I was tongue-kissing!* And then, just as things were heating up, my two friends came over and told him they wanted in on the action, too. I wasn't

We kiss again, and I realize how much I've missed just **MAKING OUT.**

jealous; I didn't really like the guy. He was simply a more-than-willing tool—it would be like getting jealous if I found someone else kissing the pole *I* practiced on. I was disappointed, though, that I had to share all the fun.

By the time we get inside and get our daughter settled, I can tell by the way my husband is looking at me that he wants more. I also know he is well aware I'm on my period, and the thought of coming inside me without a condom excites him; the mess is a small price to pay for penile freedom. What I really want is to just lie in bed and snuggle—to keep it innocent and free from the mess sex makes of us. But I can't do it. Since I have even an inkling of sexual feeling, I tell myself I should take advantage of it. We undress and start coming together, but the dark room and the smell of alcohol on my husband's breath begins to smother me. It reminds me of other youthful times when making out went too far, when it got scary and confusing, when I felt like sex wasn't really something of mine but something only for me to give away, or for others to take.

"Open your eyes," my husband says gently, breathing faster, close to coming. "I want to see you." But I can't open my eyes—if I do I won't be able to lie. I don't want him to see me now. I don't want to open that door and be real with him. I've been hiding inside the cocoon I've made for myself over the past year. Caught up with my daughter's needs, I haven't been able to see how much I'm losing myself. It's so much more than just my libido: I've lost perspective, I've lost touch with the person I was, and I've lost closeness and honesty with my husband. I was wrong; bad sex is not better than no sex, for either of us. It's just plain bad; it's disconnecting and destructive.

I need to find my way back to the good stuff, and I'm starting to get an idea of what it might take. Good sex needs to be about more than just simply opportunity or logistics, it has to. It needs to be more than hormones or raw lust or date night. It needs to be more than just charity. It starts with two people seeing each other in a real way, and each one saying to the other, *You exist, and I see you. I see you, I see you, I see you, and I still love you anyway.*

I've decided that there are some things I need to figure out: like, for starters, if I'm really dying or if I'm just a depressed hypochondriac. I'm tired of hiding things from people I love, and they're catching on to me anyway. After our last bad-sex incident, JB decided to go on a sex initiation strike. "If you want it—really want it—then you have to come get it," he said. "Maybe I'll be in the mood, maybe not." I try not to laugh when he lays this out for me. *Maybe in the mood. Ha!* It's so cute, though, that I go along with it, wishing I had a betting pool for how long he'll stick to his guns.

In the waiting room of the doctor's office my daughter is all over the place, toddling around, licking the fish tank, looking for the best germs to add to her collection of natural immunizations. I strap her in her stroller with a snack, and sigh. Apparently I've been sighing a lot lately. It's yet another thing that drives my husband crazy; he thinks I'm trying to tell him something with it. But honestly I rarely even know I'm doing it. That's actually another reason I'm here: In addition to my foggy thinking and rock-bottom libido, there are times when it feels like I can't quite catch my breath. And after my latest brain-fog fiasco—I locked my keys in the car, *with* my daughter in the car—I've decided, for her sake, that it's time to get some help. It's sad to me that I've waited this long. If my husband had these same symptoms I'd have made damn sure he went to the doctor long ago. I've made him go for lesser things. I've been so caught up in taking care of others I've forgotten how to do it for myself.

The oppressive exhaustion I battle every day is getting worse, not better, as my daughter sleeps more. I'm full of forgetfulness and weird mental mix-ups: "Have fun yesterday!" I tell the confused courtesy clerk after hearing about her upcoming birthday party. This is more than just the "mom-brain" we talk about in my mothers' group, the spaciness that results from certain mother-hormones. It's more than just the brain-dead feeling brought on by too much baby talk, and more than a dull sadness at losing the wild, carefree life I used to have.

The first time I told my doctor I was worried about being so tired, she looked at me like I was crazy and pointed to my daughter. "You have a baby," she said. "It's pretty normal." But I know it's not normal to be this tired. I watch other mothers with much more demanding children; they have three times the energy I do. I wake up with dark circles under my eyes, my face is sunken, and I have no appetite. The doctor thinks I'm probably just depressed, but she wants to run some tests anyway.

The thing is, I've had depression before, the clinical kind. And I know that right now, for all my ups and downs, I'm not depressed. Except for my physical symptoms (and apart from my worries about my relationship), I feel mostly happy and fulfilled . . . despite my generally neurotic nature, and despite some moody rough patches here and there.

Although I find the thought of being diagnosed as clinically depressed, well, *depressing,* I'm ready to do or take whatever I need to start feeling better. When I was a kid, my mom tried so hard to hide her depression from me, but I always felt it anyway. I saw through the seven-layer cakes she baked, the elaborate silk costumes she sewed for me. She didn't want to worry me, so she put on a happy face and put all her sadness aside when we were together. But the fact that she hid it made it worse for me; I worried anyway, like a pro, by myself. I'm still worrying by myself, and I'm tired of it. I don't want my daughter to grow up with the sluggish, foggy, irritable person I've become. I don't want her to think it's her job to fill me up and make me happy. I want her to feel safe enough to let go, to grow, and become everything she's meant to, without having to worry about me.

My doctor and I are both surprised by the test results that have come back: I have a moderate case of 'roid rage—postpartum hypothyroidism. At some point after the pregnancy and first year, my thyroid just pooped out on me, refusing to make enough of the good stuff that runs my metabolism. I almost laugh when I read the symptoms listed on the info sheet my doctor hands me; I know each one far too well, like houseguests who have well outworn their welcome: *fatigue* (think: dead weight), *memory loss* (think: car keys), *brain fog* (think—wait, no, don't think), *constipation* (resulting in another 'rhoid rage altogether), *irritability* (says who? Just leave me alone!), and, much to my surprise—but kind of not, too—*decreased libido* (well, hello there, stranger . . .).

I want to jump up and hug my doctor. I'm relieved to know I'm not dying or going crazy. I know that a dysfunctional thyroid doesn't explain away all the ups and downs of the past year, and that it's not going to magically turn me into Super-Sex Girl and fix what's wrong in my relationship or my life—but the discovery is a start. Certainly my thyroid is just one of many seedy characters playing a role in the case of my lost libido, but now at least one is out of the shadows. Suddenly I feel like a Cinderella story waiting to happen. I'm back in the game. And it just might be comeback time, Baby.

When I call my husband and tell him about my thyroid, it's suddenly so easy to apologize. *Sorry for being such a bitch lately. Sorry for losing my mind. Sorry for all the bad sex.* He knows as well as I do that our problems aren't just coming from my thyroid, but for now we're happy to scapegoat it. "Let me come home early and take care of you," he says, and I want to cry. I'm ready to let someone take care of me for a while. I'm open, ready for change. I feel a real metamorphosis starting. I'm becoming—but I don't know what yet.

As my daughter heads into eighteen months, she and I spend less time like lovers and more and more time like changelings. We battle for closeness and independence like some sort of horrific half beast with two heads, pushing and pulling, each trying to wrest control from the other, but still needing the other. While she sleeps I steal deep whiffs of her once-baby breath, still laced with the sweetness of my milk. I can't deny that she is becoming, too—her very own person.

Maybe my moms' group facilitator was right about finally getting my body back, about getting my groove on. I'm feeling things I haven't felt in a long time; I'm restless, unsettled, charged. I've had naughty dreams two nights in a row. The details are foggy but the sensations remind me of the dreams I had in pregnancy: deep and probing, exciting, on the edge.

Or maybe it's my thyroid medicine kicking in. I'm not normally a pill-popping kind of person (though I had been thinking lately that I could really use a mother's little helper—the Rolling Stones kind, not the teenager down the street kind), but I happily swallow my new best friend, Synthroid, every morning. Although I'm still tired in the afternoons, my brain already feels much clearer; recently, I even shocked my husband midfight by actually citing an example, a specific memory to back up my case, instead of backing out with my usual "Forget it—stop pressuring me" line. And for the first time in a long while, I can tell when I'm hungry, and I actually have the energy to eat.

With just a little of the fog gone, I can see things much more clearly. My husband is not some bulky ghost, clanking around just to annoy me. He's the same sweet guy I fell in love with, only more tired, and a little bit shell-shocked. I see my daughter as a happy, healthy little girl trying to make sense of the world—needing me, then not needing me. Holding me close, then pulling away. As much as I'd like to hold on, I can't keep her from becoming herself any more than she can make a life for me. At the park, she runs off, fearlessly tripping over her own feet, chasing a butterfly she'll never be able to catch. She gives up on the butterfly and looks back at me, teasingly. "Chase me, Mama," she says, then squeals as I take off after her.

Fall has come and nearly gone; since my husband has accrued about a million hours of comp and vacation time from hiding out at the office, and since November can be especially dreary in Berkeley, we decide it's a good time for a family vacation. Another wonderful thing about my mom's fiancé is the fact that he owns a rental condo on the Big Island of Hawaii, and true to his "is this guy for real?" nature, he's extremely generous with it.

Stepping off the plane, I'm hit with heat and memories and wet Hawaiian air. I remember visiting my mom here during one of her depressions. I remember how the sweet smell of the lei she put around my neck mixed with her cigarette smoke and coconut oil and made me feel queasy. I remember thinking how brown she looked, how healthy. My mom always felt better in Hawaii. "It's healing here," she told me. "It's magical."

Hawaii *is* magical. Almost immediately, my daughter starts treating my husband as the primary parent. The novelty of having him around full-time makes him her number one go-to guy. He's the one she wants to play with, to be held by. They splash and shriek in the pool, and amazingly I find myself with nothing to do except lie in the sun and rest. There is no laundry, because we don't wear clothes. There's very little cooking or dishes to do, because we eat out or cook fish on an outdoor grill someone else will have to scrape and clean. There's no housework, because a housekeeper comes every three days.

It makes me think that **BODYSURFING** *is not all that unlike marriage.*

At the beach, JB and I take turns playing in the waves. We get slammed and thrown and churned, not able to tell up from down, then pop back out, exhilarated. It makes me think that bodysurfing is not all that unlike marriage.

After a slightly bumpy start, our days take on a pleasing pattern:

Day one: I try to nap while my husband takes our daughter to the pool, but instead I lie awake and worry that he will let her drown.

Day two: I get up early with our daughter and we look for dolphins and whales while my husband sleeps. Later in the day, I catch him cleaning up for the housekeeper, his class sensibility offended by the idea of her doing something he could do himself.

"You treat the maid better than me," I say, joking, but my husband doesn't think it's funny; he's embarrassed and ashamed and cleans up after us for the rest of the trip, without a peep from me.

Day three: We are getting used to this. I notice, as they head to the pool together, how brown my husband is, how his skin matches the caramel skin of our daughter. I nap.

Day four: She wants only him, only his attention. "Weeve me awone!" my daughter demands, pushing me away when I try to pick her up. Her eyes light up when my husband walks in the room. "Poppy!" she yells, and barrels toward him like he's been out at sea for years. I think about being jealous, but lie on the cool marble floor of the bathroom instead.

Day five: I sit poolside reading and watch my husband and daughter play for hours in the water. I close my eyes and feel the sun on my face, filling me up, thawing me out. I think about how mothering is such a fine balance of holding on and letting go, how it's so easy to go too far one way or the other. I think about my life, and how I miss Seattle, and how I really should take that kid-friendly writing class someone told me about before we left. I think about how desperate my mom must have been to leave us on that trip to Hawaii—not knowing when or if she would be coming back, and how hard it must have been for her. Motherhood is such an easy place to lose one's footing, to get dragged out in the undertow.

Later, my husband carries our daughter up to the room and puts her down for a nap—a first. With nothing to do, nothing needing to get done, my husband and I lie on the cool marble floor together, our sun-kissed skin generating an altogether different kind of heat. The temporary relief from stifling roles, the break from housework and work stress and all the things we usually argue over, the heat and sun and ocean pounding us into submission—they've worked like a charm, reconnecting me to my husband, and to my own desires. And that connection is like a big fat On switch. I have no problem initiating right now, and I know for a fact that he's in the mood. He strips my suit off, eyes my tan line, and starts kissing my neck. As he cautiously kisses my chest, I take his hand and put it on my breast—why not? After all, Hawaii is magical; anything can happen. My husband groans in long-lost delight and kisses my nipple, gently first, then harder. He puts a hand on my other breast and teases me, whispering huskily into my ear, "Mine."

That connection *is like a big fat On switch. I have no problem initiating right now.*

Becoming Mine

For the first time in a long time, all this booby action makes me hot instead of not. And for the first time in a long time, I know I am really my own to give. I giggle and tease him back. "No way," I say, turning my lips to his as our bodies meet and become one, salty and warm and pounding like waves. "Mine."

CLIMAX

EIGHTEEN MONTHS-
THREE YEARS

SPILLPROOF LOVE

CHAPTER 5

Our society doesn't provide many role models for caring parents who are also sexual beings. We sometimes separate the two roles entirely, as though being a good mom or dad precludes you from giving great head or loving the feel of your partner's naked body next to your own.

—PAUL JOANNIDES, *The Guide to Getting It On!*

Hawaii's sweetness and magic make the return to our ordinary lives seem even more ordinary—or, as our childless friends call it, boring.

"I can't wait until we have a baby so we don't ever have to go out either," our friend Aaron chides, hungover from his going-away party—a party we once again left way too early and way too sober. We're helping him and his wife pack up their tiny apartment in San Francisco. We're not surprised that they're finally moving; they've been talking about going back to Denver for a while, finding someplace where they can actually afford a house with a yard for the dogs, someplace where they can feel good about raising the kids they want to have. It's still a blow to us, though. Not only are we losing our best (and only) backup babysitters, we're losing our best friends—friends who would come and drag us out of the house, baby and all, to go to punk-rock barbecues, or stop by and ply us with midmorning mimosas, or convince us to spend the day at the beach. They made us get dressed, put on makeup, and head back into the real world. They were always patient with our slow-moving, carseat-lugging life, but they never let us use it as an excuse to be boring. They still expected us to be us, baby and all.

The other friends I've made in Berkeley in the last couple of years are different. They are sweatpant enablers. They're masters of mom fashion, mom media, and mom commiseration. We laugh, bitch, share snacks, and have a nice time walking and having tea in sunny Berkeley backyards. It's not that I don't like them, I do. But they're as caught up in being moms as I am. It's natural that we should talk about mom stuff, after all, we met in my mothers' group, at the park, and in the Waterbabies class at the gym. But I don't know if we would be friends if our kids didn't enjoy toddling around so much together, and if we didn't have to pass the same long daytime hours together. Often I see them as a mirror I'm not quite ready to look into; when I'm with them I can't help but feel like I'm losing an important part of myself. I feel destiny tugging at my heels—a life full of muted colors and khaki clothing, a life lived for others. I know I've changed, but I still want to see myself as a tarty little creature: a little bit naughty, a little bit nice, and entirely, well, *me*. I worry that I'm getting dangerously close to becoming Monochrome Mother. I worry that I am but a small SUV away from becoming—insert horror-movie scream here—*a Soccer Mom*.

I still want to see myself as a tarty little creature: a little bit naughty, a little bit nice, AND ENTIRELY, WELL, *ME.*

My mom was definitely not a soccer mom. I don't remember her at many games, but when she did come she probably chain-smoked on the sidelines. My dad once brought rotten orange slices from the soup kitchen for a halftime snack. We were never part of a carpool because none of our seatbelts worked. I envied the soccer moms of the other girls on my team. They seemed so perfect to me; they were always perfectly coiffed, they had perfect Volvos and early model minivans. They shuttled their children to ballet and piano and birthday parties seemingly without question, didn't work outside the home, and had no apparent hobbies, desires, personalities, or teams of their own. They looked perfect, acted perfect, and appeared perfectly happy slicing snacks, or fighting stains, or hosting elaborate ice cream parties. Later, of course, I would hear of their depressions, their divorces, their affairs, their now-open closets. But at the time I envied, then hated, their apparent satisfaction. I wanted my own mom to give in to domestic motherhood as easily, to join the ranks of beige overcoats clucking on the sidelines. I wanted her to choose that life, not follow her own. I desperately wanted her to be what she could never be, and what I now worry I'm quickly becoming: a stiff. Empty. Zombie Mama.

As satisfying and fulfilling as motherhood is for me, it has knocked me right off my feet. I am out of sorts, unbalanced and unsure. On a shopping trip I'm stumped at what to buy; should I be sporty mom? Hipster mom? Sexy mom? I can't think of myself without the "mom" part thrown in there, even though on some level I still can't believe I am a mother. I'm supposed to be all grown-up, but I feel like I'm having a second adolescence: Who are my friends? What should I wear? What's that thing called sex? And what's up with my skin?

(Come on—wrinkles *and* acne?!) I'm once again, at nearly thirty-two years old, struggling to define myself, and many of the same choices are coming into play. Am I a good girl or a slut? Wild and crazy or mild-mannered? Am I the dorky, book-loving tomboy, or am I the shy, pretty girlfriend? Am I the boring, missionary position, twice-a-month housewife, or am I the lively lover, giving it to her boyfriend fast and furious in the corner of some dark alley, knowing the neighbors can hear and not giving a damn?

Even with the Synthroid, I'd hardly say my libido is back in action. I'm not nearly as tired as I was, and I feel saner and more in control, but we're definitely not bouncing off the walls like we used to. Maybe we've just outgrown that; maybe that just happens after so much time together.

My husband is going through his own changes as he tries to make sense of our sedate Berkeley life. In some ways it's everything he dreamed of—stability, safety, laughter, and warmth to come home to—but in other ways it's isolated and anemic. It's a thin, pale version of our previous lives that fits him like most of his old shirts do: a little awkward, a little uncomfortable, a little . . . tight. Although I was quick to lose my baby weight, my husband didn't have the advantage of popping out a baby to kickstart things, and now his late-night threeways with Ben and Jerry are really starting to show. "Wait up," he likes to joke, carrying Ramona in the backpack and lagging behind me on walks. "I've got this twenty extra pounds to carry . . . *and* the baby."

His new weight doesn't make him any less attractive to me, but his physical condition is an apt metaphor for this new pace of our lives: slow and deliberate, lacking energy and spontaneity. It's the bogging weight of a happy ho-hum existence, of an alternate domestic universe. In this world it's hard for me to see him as the passionate boy I fell in love with. What happened to the cocky, confident furniture mover who didn't sleep, whose skinny hipbones left bruises on me? The guy who rallied and got arrested and played Billy Bragg songs about unions and change and making a difference? The lover who wooed me (and a gathering crowd of lady onlookers) with one-armed pushups at the Gold Cane, whose veins popped when he sang, and who talked to anyone who would listen because he cared about so many things? Where did all that energy go, that life force? When he did stop challenging me, arguing with me about my bourgeois-liberal politics? And when on earth did he get so fat?

The truth is, it feels like we've traded the thin, intense versions of ourselves in for a few extra pounds of safety and comfort. We've got a kid now; we can't be as full of drama and charge as we once were. Stability is our main focus now, not spontaneity. It started out so novel, this playing-house thing, but now we're stuck in it, hooked on it, like undercover agents in way too deep. We're rogue players now, cutting off all contact with our previously naughty selves. Before all this domestic mist, my husband and I were passionate people; we lived a Technicolor life in and out of bed. Sparks flew when we were in the same room: We fought outrageously, we laughed electrically, we hummed and burned and bent like neon. We were sharp and vivid and charged. Passion was our mutual pulse: *ba-bomp, ba-bomp, ba-bomp, ba-BOOM!* That was us then.

This is us now:

"So, what do you want to do?"

"I dunno."

"We should probably have sex one of these days."

"Okay. But you're going to have to do all the work."

"Well, maybe tomorrow, then."

"Okay. Hey, what's on TV?"

I am beginning to think that television is a bigger libido destroyer than my faulty thyroid. TV gives us the sense that we're doing something together, without us really having to do anything together. It's a lot like parenthood; it's a great excuse (though not nearly as noble) to focus on something else, anything else other than what's really happening between us: no sparks, no heat, no nothin'.

Our current life is grainy and tired-feeling, sepia-toned at best. We're full of "Yes, dears," cheek kisses, even separate beds. I scoff at the magazine article that promises us "A Sizzling Sex Life" if we can just manage to sleep naked together. We can't even get the "sleeping together" part figured out, much less the "naked" stuff. My husband's snoring keeps him in the other room with the dogs, while my daughter and I inhale each other and battle it out for the big bed. It's hardly sizzling in here; it's more like Sizzler. That's how classy and exciting we are now; we're buffet-style, we're all-you-can-eat of nothing much you'd really care to. We're strip-mall, not strip-club.

After about a month's break from date night (illness, travel, exhaustion), we finally manage to pull it together again. Tonight we head into the city to see live music, something we used to enjoy together a lifetime ago—it's something we've always had in common. I'm feeling rebellious: I choose a tight, low-cut shirt that shows off my baby-mama breasts and the tattoo on my chest. I like the fact that with my husband I can dress sluttier than I would tend to going out alone; it's fun, it's naughty, but it's also safe.

I'M FEELING REBELLIOUS:
I choose a shirt that shows off my baby-mama breasts and the tattoo on my chest.

When we get to the bar, determined to rid myself of all kid thoughts, I pound two shots. It works. Walking through the crowd, I feel men's eyes following me and I smile to myself; it feels good. We weave our way through baby-faced adults so we can get up close to the baby-faced band. Everyone is beautiful and full of themselves and music and each other. I inhale the heat and energy from the crowd, sucking it down like an airborne drug. Even though he has technically quit again, my husband's smoking; I take a drag. This is as reckless and crazy as I get.

When we leave, I'm still high; the alcohol has worn off, but not the adrenaline from the music and the crowd. Not the thrill of being checked out, of being looked at like I used to, like a woman. We walk past a strip club advertising "amateur night" and I pull my husband's arm. "Wanna go?" I say, raising my eyebrows, game for some adventure, my stomach already churning with the thought. We stand in the street and stare at each other until we check the cell phone and see we've already missed two calls from my mom. "Next time," we promise each other, and head back.

By the time we get home, I'm fading. It's late, and our daughter is sleeping; we can be as naughty as we want to, and there's nothing I want to do less. My poor husband is still excited, still giving me that amateur-night look. But for me, the magic is gone. Just like that, I'm back in my old skin, back in my old role, back in my sweatpants. It's easy to see myself as sexy when other people see me that way, but after being together so long it almost doesn't count coming from my husband. I think we're so used to each other, we don't bother to look at each other with any real effort. We look toward each other, but not into each other, the way we once did. We have seen so much of each other (he has literally seen my internal organs) and have gotten so comfortable (an actual quote from him: "That haircut makes you look like Tony Danza") that we're more like brother and sister than like lovers. We don't even really fight anymore; we bicker. At least before when we fought we were passionate about something. At least we seemed to care about something other than our communal gene pool, or who got voted off of what reality show, or what kind of burritos to get. It's a friendly, familial thing we've become, but it's not sexy and it's certainly not naughty.

As much as he may want sex, my husband holds strong on his initiation strike. It's been good for us, this sexual détente. He's sticking to it, and he's not hassling me, he's not guilt-tripping me. And strangely, the more room I have to say no, the better at it I get. It's not a defensive, preemptive *no.* It's not mean, it's not wimpy, and it's not a *no* hidden inside a *yes.* It's an easier pill for him to swallow. When I curl up in his arms, he doesn't make a move on me, and soon we're both sleeping fitfully, sweating out any evidence of the evening.

I'm on BART, heading into the city for a fancy brunch where my mom is being honored for her work as a successful and socially responsible businesswoman. I'm dressed for the occasion: slightly sexy, conservatively pretty, borderline boring, until at the last minute I swap my sheer tights for nude fishnets. I like it—it's just naughty enough. I also like the looks I'm getting from men on the train. It feels good to be appreciated as a woman with no threat of sex, no built-up this or that getting in the way, just pure appreciation, pure imagination, pure long-lost sensation. Pre-sweatpant days, this kind of attention annoyed me. "Smile, beautiful," men on the train would tell me, as if I were something put on this earth for their visual pleasure, for their amusement, like a piece of art up for critique instead of a human being struggling to make it to a shitty job on time. But today, the men don't seem so piggy and gross—they're actually kind of cute. And they don't really say anything, but they do look, and I do like it. My naughty side

. . . **BUT THEY DO LOOK,** *and I do like it. My naughty side is fighting to come out again.*

is fighting to come out again, the part of me that's gotten smothered by days and days of "wife" and "mother." This is the dichotomy I have always struggled with: exhibitionist me vs. regular me. Naughty vs. nice. Seen vs. invisible. As quiet and shy as I can be sometimes, I've always craved attention. Like many women I know, I both love it and hate it. I'll never forget the way my existential philosophy professor listened sympathetically as I explained how my lack of class participation shouldn't be held against me—I was prone to panic attacks when I felt put on the spot. "Why, then," she asked, in that way that only philosophy professors can, "do you dye your hair bright orange?" *Burnt Copper,* I thought, as I left her office in a flush of bitter embarrassment. But she did have a point.

I think that's what was so sexy about the long-ago night JB and I ended up at the strip club in Vegas. The being seen. For me, seeing a naked body just doesn't kick things into gear the way it seems to for my husband; he's so visual that way. It's as if the image shoots right from his eyes to his groin, whereas for me, it's a process: I think about it, consider my feelings about it, map it, and then, *maaaybe,* it ends up in a "hot" category, but more likely it just gets filed away somewhere far from my groin, in a category like "bodies to compare mine to" or "great art I don't understand." That night it wasn't about the strippers' nakedness; it wasn't even about the thrill of being a bad girl in a strip club.

The real thrill for me that night was the way our dancer looked at me, the way she seemed to want me, the way she whispered in my ear, "I think you're cute." It was the way other men in the room watched while she straddled me, the way she kept coming back even after we ran out of money, the way she left her smell all over me, and the way my husband couldn't take his eyes off of us. It was the way I felt like I was the one on stage, I was the one everyone wanted, I was the one who mattered. That night, I was definitely *not* invisible.

The train I'm on suddenly stops and lurches backward. The lights flicker for a minute, then go completely out. With nothing to do but wait, I wistfully remember a crowded bus ride I once took shortly before I met JB, in stop-and-go San Francisco traffic. How I fell forward onto the man in front of me, innocently at first, then stayed there, pressed against this stranger, feeling his heat, his desire, his confusion. How two stops later we were even closer, my hips rubbing against his, my face in his chest, more bumping, more stopping, more going.

On a whim now, I uncross my legs and hike my skirt for the man sitting across from me. With the lights off, there's nothing to see, but I know he can sense my movement, I know he's watching—he just doesn't know what. The train jumps forward again; I put on a bored expression and recross my legs as the lights come on and we pull up to the platform.

I get off at the same station I used to for work. Although I don't miss my job, I do miss having an excuse to get dressed. I miss being downtown, being part of a city that feels alive. I miss having a pulse. I wave at the shoeshine guy who used to flirt with me while I got my morning coffee, until my pregnant belly started to show and scared him off. The bigger I got, the less he spoke to me, the less he seemed to notice me at all. It's ironic, really, the cloak of sexual invisibility that comes with pregnancy and motherhood. Here we are, walking around with teeny tiny babies or huge giant bellies, like billboards yelling HEY, WORLD, WE HAD *SEX!* And suddenly we're anti-sexy, relegated to tentlike clothes and old-lady status. Sex is what gets us into this mess, but once we're here we're treated like vestal virgins; no one wants to think of *how* we got here. They just want to see us glow and nurture and sacrifice. Walking through the BART station, I pass giant ads selling me social categories; where do I fit, which life is for me? The Victoria's Secret life, the Gap Kids life, the domestic life, the

Here we are, walking around with babies or bellies, like billboards yelling

HEY, WORLD, WE HAD *SEX!*

And suddenly we're anti-sexy.

business suit life? Regardless of the category, there are rules I've known since I was a little girl. Be pretty, society says, but not too pretty. Be smart, but not too smart. Be sexy, but not too slutty. Be visible, but not too visible. And for mothers, the ultimate expectation: Be everything, to everyone, perfectly, but with all due modesty, of course.

One of the families we lived with when I was a little kid was my godparents and their children. With my parents beginning to separate and my own mom struggling to find her footing, eventually moving into her own apartment, I worshipped my godmother as the pinnacle of homemaker-ness. She made her own baby food, kneaded her own playdough, and seemed to have endless energy for playing peek-a-boo and dealing with diapers and tears. She was exactly what I would strive to be, when I grew up, when I had kids of my own. I'll never forget when one day I found a picture of my godmother on vacation with her girlfriends. They were all sitting around naked in the hot tub, laughing, smiling in a stoned way I'd recognize later, their imperfect bodies just visible under the steam. And there she was, *smoking a cigarette*. I couldn't believe it. My perfect image of her was crushed with that one little flaw. I wanted so badly for her to be flawless—because if she couldn't be, then how was I going to pull it off as a seven-year-old?

I think that's another reason JB and I are good for each

other: He always saw me and accepted me in a way I'm just still learning to—as perfectly imperfect. He wasn't afraid to see my imperfections, and get to know them. He never put me on a pedestal (unless, of course, it was for naughty purposes) like other guys I dated had; even now that I'm the mother of his child he doesn't. When he sees me at a strip club, or in our bed, or playing in a motel mirror, I know he is seeing all of me, sagging belly and all. And he always wants me anyway.

Walking into the ballroom of the fancy downtown hotel, I worry first that I'm overdressed, then just as quickly that I'm underdressed. I'm ushered to my seat just in time to hug my mom before she gets on stage to make her speech. Up there, she is amazing, comfortably speaking to a large audience about how to make good works work. She's managed to create a successful educational software company without compromising her integrity or her values; she hires inner-city kids, she practices the socially responsible doctrine she preaches, and her software is making a difference. She's got the crowd wrapped around her finger: They laugh when they're supposed to laugh, they nod and *Hmmm* and *Ahhhh* at all the right places. She is dynamic and honest and moving. *That's my mom*, I think proudly, looking around at the faces mesmerized by the small woman with the huge personality. My mom is not perfect, not always easy—but she's always easy to admire, and to love. She's intense and unabashedly passionate; she's fierce about life, and love, and the way the world should be. And she's off the charts when it comes to charm. I remember visiting her in jail once, after she was arrested at a protest. She had already won her cellmates over, swapping stories with the prostitutes and drunks, reminding them of their humanity, their rights, the hope they once had. "The women here are amazing, honey," she garbled through the phone attached to the glass wall. "It's just so powerful."

My mom is powerful, too, but I've watched her pay a price for her charisma, her passion and power, over the years. In a very literal sense, I watched her get punished for speaking out and being the one in the spotlight, each time she got arrested for trespassing or destroying government property or not paying taxes. In a less literal sense, I watched her get punished by people turning on her, judging her. I saw the pitfalls of hippie politics, the infighting and power struggles. I noticed how people became uncomfortable when she was around; how they watched her, then jumped on any weakness she showed; how they treated her at first like she was infallible, practically holy, and then, later, when they could, like she was scandalous. This is what I learned from watching my mom: If you're a woman, attention is good, and standing out is good—just don't stand out *too* much.

Watching my mom up on the stage, suddenly I see her not only as my mom, but as a woman of her own. There's an early picture of my dad and my two-year-old brother, taken right before I was born, circa 1972. They're wearing matching three-piece suits (with psychedelic ties) my mom had sewn by hand. I can now imagine how hard it must have been for her to live that life, how smothering and overwhelming it must have felt for her at the time. I remember the elaborate cakes and costumes she used to make for me and my brother, desperate to funnel her amazing creativity. "I wonder how different things might have been if I'd had a writing group like yours when you were little," my mom said on the phone the other night, nostalgically, about the mothers' writing group I've finally joined.

My Writing About Motherhood group is a cross between a toddler playgroup, a support group, and a writing class—with a little old fashioned consciousness-raising thrown in for good measure. I found the group through a friend of a friend, thinking that I would write journal entries or cute rhyming poems about my daughter to document her babyhood. The first day, though, it was clear it was a different kind of group; it was a different kind of writing than the fluffy, joy-filled odes to motherhood I saw in the parenting magazines. It was dark and bitter and ambivalent. Since then, through our writing, we've found a way to talk about the hard stuff, the amazingly beautiful stuff, the stuff moms usually don't talk about. I'm blown away by the women in my group. Not only are they great writers but they're smart as heck. And it feels good to be challenged, to use my brain, to know that Tuesday mornings I'll have two hours to think about something other than my daughter.

The only mothers' group my mom had, way back when, she found more stifling than being at home alone. The moms sat around in perfectly kept houses, ignoring their kids, getting drunk on white wine and gossiping about other mothers and other people's desperate domestic dramas. I imagine my mom trying to change the topic from drapes to something deeper at her moms' groups, to get at some truth, to engage the intelligence of the other mothers. And I can imagine how frustrating it must have felt to her each time they just smiled and refilled her wine glass.

Now I can see how hard she must have worked to be good at her era's idea of motherhood, to fit in, to make my dad and us kids happy—even if it meant giving up her own happiness, her own life, her own passions. Now I can see how she got so lost trying to be the perfect mother and wife that she had no choice but to leave; she had to define herself outside those terms, so she to see herself as a real person of her own again, and to know she still really existed as an individual. I think maybe my mom was afraid of becoming invisible too.

Before I leave I give my mom a kiss. Seeing her so wholly is a gift, an heirloom I hope I can pass on to my daughter someday. It shows me that there is plenty of room to be me; I don't have to fake it, I don't have to break myself shooting for impossible perfection. I can be "Mother" and "other." I can be "Mommy" and "naughty."

"This is my mom," I say to anyone who will listen, showing her off as she walks me out. I know she's proud of me. I know she's showing me off, too. We're the perfect, imperfect match.

After my mom's presentation, I hop on a train to meet my husband at his office, where he has taken the baby to work with him. When I walk in, he looks up, surprised. "What's wrong?" I ask. I can't quite pin down the look he's giving me—I'm worried he's mad about something. "Did I take too long?"

"No," he says, packing up the toys strewn around his desk. "You just look really hot."

My husband decides to take the rest of the day off. On the drive home I tell him about my stop-and-go bus trip from so long ago. I was another person then: my own person, not someone's wife, not someone's mother. "What happened to that girl?" I ask him, feeling lost in all these mixed messages. We get home, and he carries our napping daughter inside and lays her on the token big-girl bed we bought after one of our last sex-related fights. My husband and I lie in our own bed together, staring up at the ceiling. "I think," he says, running a finger slowly up my leg, under my skirt, over my nude fishnets, and up farther, "that girl is still . . . right . . . here. . . . "

I can now understand that JB has never stopped seeing me as that girl. *I'm* the one who has trouble making room for her in this new life. I'm the one who's not been seeing, who's been pretending things are gone when in fact they're still right here. The truth is, I don't want to open my eyes in ten years and hate myself for letting that part of my life go. I don't want to pretend I'm something I'm not for so long that I forget how to be what I really am. I don't want to be a soccer mom, a domestic diva, a boring old nag of a pantyhose wife. I don't want to be perfect anymore, and I don't want to break myself trying to be. I want to be as whole as I can, as happy as I can, for my daughter and *for me.* I want her to grow up in a happy home, with two parents who are happy and passionate—about each other, at least, if nothing else.

I don't want to pretend I'm something I'm not for so long that I forget how to be **WHAT I REALLY AM.**

Just like that we're moving to Seattle. Not really *just like that,* more like the same way we decided to have a baby: We talked about it forever, then one day we just went for it. I worry about leaving my mom and uprooting our daughter; I worry about getting seasonal affective disorder, or falling back into the depression that drove me out of Seattle at eighteen. Mostly, though, I worry about taking JB away from his friends at work and his family. Although he goes months without visiting them, the fact that most of his family lives a short drive away is comforting to him. He's sad to leave them, but he knows it's the right thing for us. Not only are we moving into a home we'll actually own, something we never could have done here, but he sees another benefit: a potentially happier me. He knows I feel isolated in Berkeley and that I won't feel that way with my friends and family in Seattle. He also knows I'll have more help with the baby up there. But more importantly, he knows that I'll be able to find my way back to myself a little. And I can't argue with that.

At first, Seattle is paradise. We're in domestic overdrive, on a home-ownership high. We pay less mortgage now than we did for rent each month in Berkeley. We buy things like power tools and paint; we discuss the merits of stainproof vs. stain-resistant, Italian Straw vs. Almost Ivory, butcher block vs. laminate. We're living our American Dream. On top of that, JB's job is letting him keep his position and telecommute from home, which means my daughter and I get to see a lot more of him. Actually, everyone in the neighborhood does, as he's taken to not getting dressed for work beyond boxers and an undershirt. The weekend naptime we used to so carefully reserve for sex (or, more realistically, for fighting about sex) suddenly is a moot point.

Early on into parenthood we pretty much gave up on nighttime sex; our daughter was always in the bed, I was tired and cranky, or our shows were on. With JB at work all day, and our daughter waking up before us, weekend naptimes were our one big shot; we worked our sex life around the weekend hours of 1–3 PM, which just ended up causing more fights because of the pressure. But now we're giddy: "Every day has *naptime*," my husband gloats over the phone, calling me from his office downstairs. When I walk by to do laundry, he gives me a big thumbs-up through the old-fashioned glass door. We christen each room of the house. We have lots of barbecues and big dinners with old friends. We sit on the porch with our neighbors from across the street, the very people who sold us our house—one of them is an old girlfriend of mine from childhood. We drink wine and talk about old times and new times and the neighborhood while our daughter sleeps soundly inside. Later, we let them watch her while we sneak down to the County Line, two blocks away, for beers and karaoke. It's just like the good old days, watching JB bring down the house with his super-high-energy version of the Animals' "We Gotta Get Outta This Place." We're blissfully happy with our new, homey life. *Maybe we just needed a new start*, I think as we hold hands and sing along to "I Got You Babe" with the lesbian truck drivers who live down the block.

Before long, though, domestic bliss wears off, and we've settled right back in. With no commute time for my husband, my days with my daughter are considerably shorter, but they're not really all that different. Most of my friends work during the weekdays, so I'm off to the zoo with my nephews, or to the tots' swim class at the Y, or to the park with the neighbors. There's still laundry; there's still TV and burritos and exhaustion at the end of the day. There's still are arguments about who does what and how often, and about what we do during naptime. And I'm still not sure how to make sense of it.

My husband isn't much better off. I notice that with no office to go to, he mostly doesn't shave and spends quite a bit of time hairy and half-naked and just a little insane-looking. He's always been the more social one, and without coworkers or local friends of his own I think he's going stir-crazy. He spends more and more of his free time at the local coffee shop, slamming lattes and chatting up the baristas, who, as far as I can tell, are all women, and cute, and young. The days I join him, I feel frumpy and outdated. I may have traded my sweatpants for jeans and my slippers for a pair of Pumas, but let's face it, I'm still wearing a mom uniform. I'm not really jealous of the girls; they just make me sad. It seems they're more like *me* than I am these days.

A couple months after moving, we're settling in for the night when my friend across the street calls to see if she can bum a smoke from my husband, who has not-so-secretly taken up smoking again with his coffee shop friends. "I'll be right back," my husband whispers as I wrestle our daughter into bed. Two hours later, he's still not home. I call across the street, but no one answers the phone. I peek out the door and see lights on at another neighbor's house. I don't want to leave my daughter alone, so I pick her thirty-five pounds up and throw her over my shoulder with a blanket, then shuffle down the street, barefoot and crazy-haired in sweatpants. Halfway up to the house, I hear people talking in the backyard. I hear my husband's booming, charismatic voice as he finishes a funny story I've heard a million times. He's in his element. I hear everyone laughing and loving him and handing him more beers. I want to scream. Standing there, in the middle of the street with my daughter slung over my shoulder, like a madwoman with a sack of potatoes, I hate him. I think about knocking on the door and telling him to come home, but I've never met these neigh-

I hear everyone laughing and loving him and handing him more beers.

I WANT TO SCREAM.

bors before. I don't want to be all *COPS* or *Jerry Springer* about it, knocking on their door in my skivvies, eyes wide and crazy: *Where's my damn husband, bitch!* Instead, I lug my daughter home and watch *Oprah* reruns until he comes home, oblivious. "What's the matter?" he says, smelling guiltily like socialization, honestly unsure why I look like I'm about to kill him.

"What the fuck is wrong with you? I had no idea where you were!" I shout, unleashing hours of pent-up anger. "You said you were coming right back!" He's so clueless, though, that I run out of steam and start crying. "Why didn't you call? Why didn't you ask me to come over, too?"

"I don't know," he says lamely, getting lamer. "I guess I just thought you wanted to be here, you know, at home." *Want to be here? Like I'm not here all fucking day? Like I have no other interests, no desire to speak to other adult human beings? This is what he thinks of me now,* I think. *He thinks I'd rather be at home watching reruns than hanging out with him and meeting new people.*

"How do you think that makes me feel?" I cry. I'm pushing it now. I know he hates it when I cry, and I can tell he's genuinely sorry, but I can't stop. "It's like I don't even matter to you, like you don't give a shit about me anymore."

At a loss, he struggles to find the right response. "Oh, no, baby, no," he says, wrapping his arms around me. "Just today I was watching you guys play in the yard and it was amazing. I'm so fuckin' lucky. You're an amazing mom. You two are my life."

He's so damn sweet, and so damn dumb. In full self-pity mode, I launch another attack. "I don't want to be 'you guys'! I don't want to be an 'amazing mom'! I want you to give a shit *about me* because of just me. Me, the woman you married, not all this crap." I kick at the vacuum cleaner to make my point. I'm all worked up, I'm frustrated, and I'm hurt. I feel like a neurotic, trapped housewife, a robot wife malfunctioning. But that's the real problem here. That's not the way he sees me; it's the way I do. I'm off-kilter, pulled too far into self-centeredness by this mother-induced state of disequilibrium. I'm self-absorbed in a hysterical, insecure way, like a teenage girl lost in the drama of a prom-ending pimple.

After our fight, I can't sleep. I get out of bed and find my husband raiding the fridge. He passes me the ice cream, and we sit quietly in the dark, sharing a spoon, swapping bites like compadres, siblings pulling off an ice cream coup while their parents are away. We're stuck here in sweet and cool, between who we were and who we're trying to be. We want so badly to make this work, to get it right. We're starving for the connection we once had, but we're so busy just trying to get by that we're missing it.

And lately I find I'm getting hungry in another way. I thought that with the introduction of my husband's sex initiation strike I would go for months without getting turned on, without thinking about sex. But it's not happening like that. I'm shocked by the warmth I feel in the UPS guy's hands, and by the strange desire I have to rub my hands over my mechanic's dark, suddenly magnetic face. I like the way my daughter's young swim instructor stands too close to me without knowing it. I like his baby face, his skinny body that smells like chlorine (and nothing else). I like how he gets nervous when I sit with the kids at the edge of the pool. I like how he shivers. It's been a long time since I've made someone shiver. I want to make someone shiver.

I like how he gets nervous when I sit with the kids at the edge of the pool.

I LIKE HOW HE SHIVERS.

Maybe tonight I'll get my chance. JB and I are celebrating our ten-year anniversary: five years of being married, and five years as lovers before that. My dad has agreed to take our daughter for the evening and has strict instructions not to bring her back until after ten. It's not quite the fantasy I had hoped for. Desperate to bring back some shiver and spark, I had hoped we would be in Vegas. I had hoped for a weekend of naughtiness, of drive-through vow renewals, of drunken, dark fantasies. But domestic devotion won again: At 2 PM on Friday our daughter seemed no more ready to be left for a weekend than she was as a newborn.

That afternoon I consoled myself with a trip to Victoria's Secret, the self-proclaimed naughty headquarters of the world. While my daughter flirted with the saleswomen, most of whom looked like children themselves, I confessed my plans to surprise my husband with a burst of anniversary sexiness. They all thought it was such a cute idea—at least until I discreetly asked (after seeing the price of panties that were just going to come right off), "Got any crotchless?"

You would think I'd asked where the **INFLATABLE SHEEP** *section was.*

You would think I'd asked where the inflatable sheep section was. Their disapproving looks made me feel like a cheap whore of a mother. I tried to make up for it by buying too much and having my daughter say something cute and charming as we left, as if that would prove I was still a good mom.

I drop Ramona off at my dad's, and get home with time to shower. I even muster up the energy to shave my armpits, which are well beyond European chic at this point. I put on my new black bra and garter, minus panties, and feel vindicated. It looks better pantiless anyway. Screw those nubile youngies with their tunnel vision, their mother/whore complexes. I'm tired of letting other people define my sexuality—Victoria's Secret, ass-noting boys, *whore*-calling girls, dumb boyfriends, stupid TV shows. Why shouldn't I have my cake and jump out of it, too? I think about the look on my husband's face as he takes off my skirt. The thought makes the swim instructor seem like a child. A fop. I laugh at the thought.

We eat meat and chocolate under a canopy in our yard. There are no veggies. There is no fight about how many bites to have. We drink champagne and talk about getting remarried in Las Vegas; we write down vows and read them to each other, tell stories, reminisce.

"Remember that one night in Reno?" I ask, and my husband nods, eyeing the shirt I've unbuttoned more than usual to show off my new bra. Of course he does. In Reno we role-played; I dressed up like a prostitute and met him at the bar downstairs. On the way up to our room, we stood on opposite sides of the elevator, with a stranger between us. By the time the door opened all three of us were sweating; the heat and tension of the ride was palpable. In our room, we acted out a fantasy without ever talking about it beforehand, without any awkwardness. We were so close and connected, anything went. At the time, my husband was distraught about having just visited his brother in prison and he just needed to be taken care of; what he couldn't ask for in "real" life he asked me for that night. So I took care of him, like a professional, all night. Riding him, teasing him, wearing him down until all he could think about was me, until all he could do was me. Again and again until morning, when I held his head in my arms and we both finally slept.

Through the walls we could hear the neighbors, making the whole thing even hotter and naughtier, and we responded in kind with our sounds, uncut, unedited. We didn't censor or judge—each other, or ourselves. There was only passion and heat and red hotel walls.

Downstairs we play. I try to create our own little Vegas by stripping for JB, but I trip clumsily in my heels over toys that never got put away. I giggle, and head upstairs for more wine. As I brush past my husband, he spins me and kisses me hard. "You're my wife," he whispers. "My wife." There's something about the way he says it that makes me melt under the weight of the words. He pulls me down, right there, on the stairs I carry laundry up, in the house we've made a home in. My dual roles abruptly feel irresistibly hot. I wouldn't trade our boring closeness for anything; there's a freedom in it, a safety that'll open all kinds of naughty doors if I just let it. I tackle him on the carpeted stairs, knocking over his glass of wine in the process. For a moment, we freeze. I fight off the urge to gather my force of cleansers and attack the stain; it's time to put away the housewife for the night, time to cut those ol' apron strings. We're both relieved when I laugh, and opt, instead, to attack him.

"It's okay," I whisper as he pulls up my skirt and grabs at the garter, "it's spillproof."

Self-Love in Seattle

CHAPTER 6

WEAN *(wēn) tr.v.* **WEANED, WEANING, WEANS**
1. *to accustom (the young of a mammal) to take nourishment other than by suckling.*
2. *to detach from that to which one is strongly habituated or devoted.*

—*The American Heritage Dictionary of the English Language,* fourth edition

At two and a half, my daughter starts to wean herself. Any emotional or hormonal stability I've developed over the past year flies out the window—I'm thrown into udder insanity, hormonal hell. I'm all over the map, crying at TV commercials one minute, lusting after nineteen-year-old boys the next. It's a motherly kind of lust, though; I want to pull their low-rider pants up, spank them for being punks, then put them to my breast and either nurse them or fuck their brains out. It's unsettling. Worse than the hormones, though, is the intimacy withdrawal that comes with my daughter's growing autonomy. "Get *outta* here, Mama," she berates me when I come into the room. She pulls away when I reach for her, she squirms when I move to kiss her. I want to pull her close, rein her in, desperate to keep the perfect oneness we had when she was a baby. But she's got different plans. My daughter's eyes mirror what I feel: fear and intoxication. Independence looms over every interaction: a lure, a shadow, the terror and thrill of freedom. I try to turn my back on it, but I know it's there, undeniable, firm, always knocking.

"She's so independent," the preschool teacher says as my daughter pushes me out the door. I want to snatch her back, scoop her up, and run home and lie in bed all day, snuggling and nursing like we did just months ago. All the way to school she'd chatted semi-incoherently about what she's learned about caterpillars, butterflies, cocoons. She's a tiny know-it-all. I want to grab her shoulders and set her straight: *I know a thing or two about butterflies, too,* I want to say. I want to tell her about the time her dad tried to take me out, to loosen me up and reorient me to the world of grownups, when all I could think of was her and the butterflies she delighted in. *I know a thing or two about butterflies. And cocoons.*

In many ways, I'm weaning, too. Not just from the postpartum hormones I've become accustomed to, the delicious warm rush of the "love drug" oxytocin, the sharp, satisfying feel of my milk letting down. But I'm also weaning myself from full maternal absorption, from what's been filling me up the past two and a half years, from the nourishing and compulsive effects of what feels to me like a biological imperative: attachment, bonding, connection. Coming out of this foggy chrysalis, I'm hungry for everything. I want to eat my daughter, send her back inside me where we'll always be close, we'll always be one. I'm hungry for chocolate and salt and the fantasy of running off with a stranger. I'm hungry for my husband when he's not around, and then suddenly, when he is, I'm hungry to be left alone. I troll the aisles of Target: What will it be? Where's my good thing? Where's my pacifier? Where's that perfect something I'm looking for? Is it a new duvet cover? A Big Hunk candy bar? A ten-dollar, funky-fitting Made in China shirt that I'll take back tomorrow?

I am hungry for everything . . . *What will it be? Where's my good thing? Where's my pacifier?*

Self-Love in Seattle

I blow Ramona a kiss and wave to her through the painted preschool window. As I head off, unsure how to spend my free time, I curse my mom for her generosity; she's the one who started this, offering to pay for my daughter's preschool two mornings a week. *Room for You,* it says under "Memo" on the check my mom sends each month in the mail. But I'm not sure I want a room of my own. Theses days I know how to do "we" a whole lot better than I know how to do "me." With time to breathe, I feel lost. With time for me, I feel like a fake. After all, I'm now the stay-at-home mom of a kid who isn't even at home two mornings a week. What kind of Supermom is that?

Across the street, I walk into a children's consignment store to browse. I pick out some size three pants, but they look enormous. I hang them back up and touch the baby clothes on my way out; the onesies, the footsies, the tiny little dresses with tiny matching hats. Just looking at them makes my breasts ache, my hormones surge. Here it comes. I'm suddenly awash in hysterical longing, newborn-lust, *Invasion of the Baby Makers.* I'm practically drooling. Then, just like that, the swell recedes. I'm sane again. I watch with a combination of horror and envy as a mom walks into the store, corralling and shushing her rowdy toddler, her arms full of her sleeping second, desperate to distribute her energy and attention with motherly fairness. Although part of me wants to be in that club—to know I can do it, to earn my wings and get that prestigious two-kid street credibility—another part of me knows that for me it's a dangerous flirtation. Because, for me, fresh mother-love is the stickiest, grabbiest, most desperately satisfying kind of love; it is tireless and amnesia-inducing. It makes me forget I ever desired anything else, or ever dreamed different kinds of dreams.

By the time I get home, I have an hour and a half before it's time to pick up my daughter. It's too much time, and never enough. It's too much time to spend on housework, and it's too little time to start working on my new writing project: a sex (or lack thereof) column for moms (*that's right—give me some material, baby!*). Although I no longer have the real-time support of my writing group, I'm still active with them online; I'm an editor and columnist for the online magazine *Literary Mama*. I didn't plan on writing about sex—it just kind of happened. *Why not write a sex column?* I thought. At the very least it will give me an excuse to read up on the topic; at the very best it will give me an excuse to actually *do it*. It's a great gig, though it's had some drawbacks; suddenly everyone wants to tell me every private detail about his or her sex life ("Ew—I can't *hear* you, Mom!"), not to mention my husband has new ammunition against any prudish tendencies of mine, teasingly threatening to out me to my fans as not actually being very naughty.

I blow both things off, and take a long shower instead. I

shave, I exfoliate. I step out lightheaded, the heat and freedom conspiring. I call downstairs, where my husband's at work, and ask him if he can take his lunch yet. "I'll be up in a minute," he shouts. But I have other, naughtier plans. I walk naked into his office, unbutton his pants, and sit on his lap. "I want to make you happy," I say, slipping him inside me for a rare, condom-free moment. After a minute, he pulls back out teasingly and begins kissing me. "And what can I do for you?" he asks, fingering my hip, eyebrows arched, playful, committed. "What is it that *you* want?"

And this is the question. What do I want. What do I want? *What . . . do . . . I . . . want?*

The romance is instantly gone. What I want right now, more than anything, is for him to not ask me that question. To stop being so damn sweet and generous, to stop staring at me, stop trying to find me, stop trying to please me when I don't even know who *me* is anymore. What I really want, now, is to be left alone.

"Will you just fuck me already, please?" I snap as I get up and throw him a condom from the closet. It works. He gets the message and starts walking out of the room, hurt. "You know," he says, stepping over the unused condom and setting a mine of his own on the way out, "you really ought to get a life."

He's right, of course. I need more than just a room of my own; I need a life of my own. A life with room to coax my libido out of the shadows, where a couple of raw words won't send it back into hiding.

The next day my daughter and I are both prickly and moody, and it's not a school day. "I need 'pace," she says, slamming her door after some unforgivable act of mine, like trying to help her put her shoes on. With this new attitude, it seems like she should be turning thirteen soon, not three. The problem with getting a break from my daughter a couple days each week is that when I don't get that break, I know exactly what I'm missing. It's similar to my relationship with chocolate; I can go weeks without it, but the minute I have just a taste, I suddenly can't get enough. It's almost easier to just go without.

Stuck in the house, both of us struggling with issues of independence, my daughter and I are over-involved with each other. There's no new baby or older sibling to mediate the intensity between us. There's nothing else to focus on. I wish we could go back to the beautiful backpack days, walking and laughing and basking in oneness under the bright Berkeley sun. But we're in another place now, here in Seattle we're in the Great Gray, the soupy wet thick of things, and we're both trying to spread our wings.

Desperate, at least for the moment, for some space of my own (maybe I really do need that room), I set my daughter up with a video and bowl of dry cereal and go in the other room to check my email. After a while, I *know* she's too quiet out there, but I kind of just don't care. I take the time, for myself, and decide I'll deal with any consequences later. When I do come out, I find her lying naked in a mess of cereal; she's dumped her bowl all over the couch, all over her body, and is currently rubbing it all around the outside of her "bagina," her new favorite body part. At first I'm mad about the mess on the couch, and then I'm mad that she has broken the awkwardly established set of rules we've created around this new fascination of hers, rules that include statements like "Sand is for digging, not putting in your pants" and "Toothbrushes are for teeth, not *vaginas.*"

I stand there, ready to launch into a reminder of those rules, when suddenly I falter. I want my daughter to be positive and clear about her body, for her to know and trust the goodness in herself, but for some reason every time I say the word *vagina,* I notice a strange cascading lilt to my voice, a halting and falsely positive pitch normally reserved for questionably fun concepts like *babysitter* or *long car ride.* I don't know where this lilt comes from. I certainly didn't grow up with it. My mom, determined to raise a sex-positive young girl, said *vagina* not with a lilt, but with the ferocity of a two-year-old snatching back a stolen toy. She taught me the word *clitoris* at the same time that she taught me *belly button, toes,* and *elbow.* Even today she shines when she tells the story of how at just barely two years old, in the middle of Mass, I cried out, "Mommy, these overalls are pinching my clitoris!"

My mom claims to have been embarrassed, but deep down I think she must have thought my tiny voice, stating so clearly my tiny needs, was a kind of miracle. I can only imagine the sex education she got growing up in an Irish Catholic family with four boys, a stern—if loving—sick mother, and an alcoholic father. I imagine the nuns who raised her, so quick to write off her intelligence, her passions, her individuality, were also quick to tell her what they thought she needed to know: *Stop sinning. Get married. Make babies. Be quiet.*

My own sex education was far more extensive; my dad and stepmom loaned books on the topic to my fifth grade class, and by the time I was sixteen my mom had taken me out to brunch for a "woman-to-woman" talk. She knew I had a boyfriend and that things were getting serious. She talked to me about taking care of myself. About being sober. About using two types of birth control. About getting on the pill, when I was ready. And then, over tea and croissants and coun-

And then, over tea and croissants, my mom said, "Honey, I want to **buy you a vibrator."**

try cheese, my decidedly hip and unshy mom grabbed my hand, pulled me close, and said, "Honey, I want to buy you a vibrator."

As it turns out, of course, I had already had sex, and I wasn't sober at the time. I hadn't used protection, and I certainly didn't want anything to do with a vibrator. Despite my parents' valiant efforts, I wasn't the sexually self-assured young woman I should have been.

And now it's my turn, and here I am, lilting. Unsure. Worried about the effect my choice of words and tone will have on my not-even-three-yet daughter's sexual future.

I finally decide to take a neutral, casual approach with my daughter. I sit down next to her on the couch and ask, simply, "Well, how does that feel?"

For a second she scowls, annoyed that I've interrupted her movie. But then she turns, gives me a big toothy smile, and announces shamelessly: "Perfect!"

I know I'm hormonal and out of sorts because I'm weaning her, but it makes me terribly sad that my daughter seems to know more about herself, more about what makes her happy and what feels good to her, than I do, nearly thirty years her senior. I'm just learning, now, in fits and starts, what she naturally knows. I sit and watch the rest of the movie with her, and sniff away tears at the happy ending. After that, I help her get cleaned up and we head out for a swim at the gym. There's a break in the rain, and a boost in our moods. And, of course, we both always benefit from the attention the young aquatic department gives us.

Showering side by side in the locker room, I watch my daughter before we head to the pool. She looks absurd in the two-piece suit she's wearing, its teenage cut underscoring her huge milk belly. I imagine, for a minute, the day she asks me to buy her a thong.

In the pool she tests her new independence; with her float belt on she paddles away from me, floundering but determined. She plays on the wall with another little girl while I test my own new independence, once again flirting with the instructor, who this time is leading a triathlon training class for adults. "You should sign up," he says. "I can help you with your stroke."

Last year my sister-in-law did the same minitriathlon as a "getting her body back" thing, three months after giving birth to her second son. And another older mom friend just climbed a mountain to "reclaim her body"—thirty years after the birth of her daughter. Although I like the idea of taking my body back, I was quite frankly leaning more toward something a little more decadent—and something requiring a little less, um, work. Like taking up smoking again, or going to the spa. At the moment it's suggested, though, my happy hormones lead the charge and I feel much more noble. "Sign me up," I flirt back, and pretend not to notice my swim top coming a little too loose.

Later that week my husband and I go out separately for the night. With my dad babysitting, my husband goes out for a beer with a new potential friend, the father of one of our daughter's preschool playmates. It's awkward, I've noticed, this men-making-friends thing. The two of them get along well at school functions and dinner parties, but what's the next step? How does one grown man ask another for a playdate sans wife and kid? By the time they've figured out a way to drink beer together, the man's wife and I have already become fast friends; we've jumped in the neighbor's hot tub together, naked. We've met each other's family and friends. I know she likes to have her toes sucked. But that's women, I guess.

Although my husband is one of the most social people I know, for some reason he's acting like his social life is unimportant these days, as if videos and burritos are all he needs to be happy. I think he's so relieved that life is boring and safe and eight hundred miles away from the drama of his family that he's afraid to push his luck and ask for anything more. He's great at surviving life, but not always so great at thriving at it. "Sometimes," he said the other day, seemingly out of the blue, "I feel like I'm just passing time, trying to make it until I die without any more drama or major bumps." I guess I'm not the only one who needs to get a life. At the time I kissed him and held his head, but I wasn't sure what to say. In truth, I was a little pissed. I don't want him to be happy with the bare minimum, content with watching TV and being withdrawn and lackluster. I'm a loving hypocrite; I want him to be the side of me that I can't be. I want him to remind me we're still alive, still in the land of the living. He's cocooning now, too, and I don't know how to handle it. I'm so caught up in my own slow metamorphosis that I don't want to see his. It's another mirror I'm not ready to look into. It makes me nervous and idiotic and for some reason way too chipper. "Well, that doesn't sound like very much fun," I answered lamely, and fled to the store to buy him ice cream.

The same night he has his "man-date," I meet my girlfriends at our favorite local bar. It's dark and quiet by the time I head out. With no daughter and no husband I feel like I'm twelve again, sneaking out to meet the very same girls. We've been friends since second grade, and have seen each other through all kinds of firsts and lasts. It amazes me that after all this time we still have things in common.

In the car I drive fast and listen to loud music that makes no references to farmers or dells or sunshine. When I get there, at ten, the place is hopping. I take a seat at the bar and wait for my friends. It feels good to be out at night, *alone.* I smile at the cute bartender, something stirring in me; I admire his muscular forearms as he pours my drink, and watch the way he works the ladies and the money and the crowd. Before I know it, the crowd has thinned out and the cute bartender is leaning toward me on his cute forearms; we exchange our names over loud music. "So, then, what do you do, Heidi?" he ask-flirts, using my name like he already knows me, or like he wants to know me. It's a simple question, but I'm utterly befuddled. Two and a half years of mother-love stupor renders me useless and empty in this foreign environment. I lean forward and stutter, "I'm a homemaker," the ancient word sticking bitterly to my tongue. For a minute he is confused. In this industrial, arty crowd, he actually thinks I make homes. Build homes. But a moment later he gets it, and a moment after that we're both relieved when my friends show up and we move to a table at the back of the bar.

When I get home I can't stop thinking about the bartender. I'm learning the problem with having a life above and beyond sweatpants: It can be dangerous. It's easy to dive into domesticity when you feel like that's all there is, when it becomes your whole life. It's a lot harder when you realize there's a whole world still out there, when you realize there are other choices you can make, and that maybe you've left something vital behind. It's been much safer for me to just keep those doors closed, to turn those adventurous parts of myself off. But now I wonder what else I've lost by doing that—what else might have gotten turned off. . . .

I find my daughter asleep in her new, mostly still unused big-girl bed in her room, and my husband asleep in our grown-up bed. I strip and get under the covers next to him. I can tell he feels my body against him and is waking up. In the dark room we come together slowly, without saying a word. I give up on trying to get the bartender off my mind, and just decide to go with it. I close my eyes and picture myself on top of him, the way his arms might flex as he grabs me and moves me slowly up and down. I roll on top of my husband and kiss him, open-mouth, with tongue, like I would kiss a stranger, the way I did the night we met. In the shadows I can't see his face, and I don't want to. I'm suddenly very wet. My nipples graze my husband's chest and I imagine the bartender's quirky little smile, the way his body might pulse touching mine for the first time, the way he might be shocked at my tired, beautiful, worn body. The way he might not be able to stand it. I get wetter. My husband puts on a condom and slips inside me. Unlike with a stranger, or the bartender, there's nothing for me to worry about—no remorse,

I roll on top of my husband and kiss him, like I would kiss a stranger, the way I did THE NIGHT WE MET.

no ruined family, no weirdness. We shimmy and shake and slide around the bed, around the room like we used to, until we're both all used up, both exhaustedly satisfied. "Wow," my husband says, lying sideways, kissing my arm. "Well, I guess you had a good time out tonight."

Here's a confession: Although I have no problem with the occasional erotic reverie (um, hello, swim instructor), I have very little experience actually fantasizing during sex. I know enough about sex to know it's fine and healthy to do so. I know my husband does it; he's got an active fantasy life he's never afraid to share with me, and I like it when he does. (His fantasies are not all that complicated. They all start the same way: "Okay, it's me and you and these two strippers . . . ") I don't get jealous over it; usually, I just get hot. I like to know what he thinks is sexy, and it's a way we can talk about sex without having to actually sit down and talk about sex. But for some reason, when it comes to my own fantasies, I'm stumped. It's not only that I get carried away in the details (*wait—what clothes would I be wearing? And where's our daughter? What about birth control?*), it's that I guess in some way I always worry that if I think about someone else during sex, then it must mean I'm unhappy. It must mean, I think, that there's something wrong with *us;* it must mean the magic is over. It's cause for panic. *Oh my god, I must have chosen the wrong man! I should have waited for Johnny Depp after all!*

But after this latest bartender-enhanced sex, I'm starting to sing a different tune. In the hunt for the lost libido, I'm finding, anything goes. Maybe it's not the end of the world to fantasize about another man; maybe it's the beginning of a new one.

My husband wakes up in the morning energized. He feels connected, and I think more hopeful. Since we've stopped having bad sex, our good sex just keeps getting better. He's much happier with less when the sex we do have ends up like it did last night. He kisses me and happily takes our daughter out for pancakes, leaving me to rest. I'm so tired, but I have a hard time falling back asleep; I'm still not used to sleeping without my daughter right there. She's become my security blanket in so many ways over the past couple years. It's getting harder and harder to deny that I'm the one with separation anxiety. I'm the one who is still needy and hungry, the one who's afraid to really let go and get a life of my own.

I'm hungover from lack of sleep and the cigarettes I smoked at the bar. I decide smoking is definitely *not* the way to go. Especially after the *Oprah* I saw the other day, with the cute doctor who showed us the damaged, black insides of real lungs from smokers who'd died. Come to think of it, that same doctor was the one who said that for optimal health we should strive to have something like two hundred orgasms per year.

I'm certainly not there yet, but it seems to me as good a goal as any—more fun than a triathlon, at least.

Lying there, head aching, feeling wound up and strung out on weaning and post-sex hormones, I think of an old boyfriend who swore by the healing effects of sex as a hangover cure. *Hmm. Well, why not?* Since there's no one else around, I start to touch myself. I can't believe how long it's been since I've done it—what happened to that staple of my childhood and teen and pre-husband years? It's not that I don't know how to pleasure myself; just recently my husband caught me in the shower, eating my private stash of peanut M&M's. But masturbation hasn't occured to me for months—wait, no, *years.* I try to think of the last time I touched myself for pleasure's sake, but I can't even remember the last time I was in bed alone before today. Even if I had been inclined to get myself off, it would've felt horribly impractical. I've gotten so used to multitasking that the idea of getting off without my husband screams of shameless inefficiency. Somehow over the years self-pleasure has become something *for him*, or *for us*, but never just *for me.*

Even if I had been inclined to get myself off, it would have felt HORRIBLY IMPRACTICAL.

I lie in my bed alone and think back to the bartender. I touch myself in the way I would want him to kiss me: slippery, slowly at first, faster. Suddenly I feel exposed, and embarrassed; I get up to make sure the shade is all the way down, then climb back in bed and try to act casual. *What's the big deal? What kind of sex columnist can't make herself come? What kind of example am I setting? And why on earth can't I say* vagina *without lilting?* I glance over at the window and finally start to relax. I think of the bartender and imagine him touching himself, at home in bed, while he thinks of me. I gain momentum. *See, I'm still naughty.* I can still get some excitement and thrill from my very first lover: myself.

When I come, it's different than how I do with my husband; it's more external, more like an exercise, and in some ways it's an easier release. It feels good. What do you know? That ex-boyfriend was right. I feel better, and I probably burned some calories in the process. I close my eyes, open up, and do it again.

A couple weeks later, my husband and I arrange to have a whole day together by ourselves. We drop our daughter off at my dad's for a babysitting marathon and head to our first stop: Toys in Babeland, a woman-friendly sex shop. One benefit of writing a sex column is that on my birthday, instead of getting new socks from my family, I got a big fat gift certificate to this place.

As we head into the store, my husband puts him arm around me and says, "Let's get you a vibrator," in the same generous tone he would use to say, "Let's get you a massage," or "Let's get you a night off." I can tell he's pleased with himself. "You know, *for you*," he says, giving me his best come-hither.

Great, I think as we walk in the store, s*omething else to clean.*

We roam around the store a bit together, pointing out the more unique toys: a male chastity belt ("Isn't that an oxymoron?"), a full leather bondage harness (Naughteeee!), something called the "Little Flirt buttplug" (no comment—I once was under the mistaken impression my husband wanted a little more action in the back, and when I learned slightly too late that he didn't, we were fortunate enough to be able to laugh it off with minimal damage), and various dildos mounted on walls, with names like "Big Red" and "Mr. Bendy." ("I think I had a pet named that!") After a bit, we drift our separate ways. I head to the media section, and my husband, trying to look more at ease than he feels, gravitates toward the wall of condoms. Despite the fact that I'm in a sex store, with sex, sex, sex everywhere, it's not until I pick up a book of erotica that I start warming up and feeling less awkward, and it's not until I notice the cute lipstick lesbian checking me out that I really start getting a little thrill.

It's ironic that I'm so out of touch with my fantasies, since my whole sexual life got started in my imagination—thanks especially to my favorite tattered library copy of Judy Blume's *Forever.* That book's sweet, clean boy-girl scenes were so much more attractive to me than the dirty pictures in the *Playboy* I found under my brother's bed. I've always needed a story to get turned on. It isn't seeing something sexy, or having the right someone do the right something to me, that gets me hot (though don't get me wrong, those things certainly aren't bad); it's all about me, really. About the real or made-up emotional involvement I have with someone, the real story behind who we are and why we're together and what we (desperately, hungrily) need from each other.

I pick up another book and lean against the wall when I'm hit by a miniature hot flash; I flush, and notice how full my breasts still feel. I wonder if I'm ever going to be *post*-postpartum. I go to put the book down and bump hands with the lipstick lesbian. "Oh, sorry," I fumble, like I'm twelve and she's a boy. For all I know, I have the same burgeoning hormones running through me now that I had back then; they feel as out of control. And my own body, though much more experienced, feels strange and foreign to me in the same way. I smile shyly, clutching my book, and head over to check out the vibrators.

I meet up with my husband at the checkout counter. Ever the practical one, he hands me a Costco-size bottle of lubricating jelly. *Hope springs eternal,* I think, then suddenly I feel claustrophobic and ready to go.

"So what are you going to get?" JB asks wryly, slyly, not-a-hint-of-shyly. I show him the books I've picked out, along with a small "Rub My Ducky" vibrator that looks just like a real rubber ducky. "For the bath," I say. I like that it's disguised. It's like me: cute, yet naughty.

"That's it?" he says, and pulls me back over to the vibrators. "What about this one?" He points to a giant metal contraption with dials and switches. It brings to mind an email that I saw a while back—a cartoon picture captioned "The Difference Between Men and Women." Under the word "Men," there was a picture of a simple On/Off light switch. Under "Women," there was a supercomputer, a huge contraption with all kinds of different plugs and buttons and hoses.

I look up at my husband's eager face as he holds up this particular complex machine, and wistfully remember an email from a fan who complained to me about her husband getting jealous of her vibrator. *Why can't that be my man?* I wonder. *Why does he have to be so damn thoughtful?*

"I don't know. It's just so . . . big," I say.

My husband looks exasperated. "Okay, what about this one?" He asks, pointing to something else. I start to get annoyed. "No—leave me alone," I say. "I want my ducky. I like him. He's cute. I thought this was for me, anyway."

My husband shoots me back a nasty look. I can't believe we're going to get in a fight—on our day off, at the sex store—about which vibrator I should want. I'm hungry and cranky and stuffy and hot. I look at the clock and see that an hour of our precious alone-time is gone. *When are we even going to have time for sex?* I think. *Great.*

"Why don't you get it *for you,*" I whisper, "if you want it so bad? Why does every fucking thing have to be about me and my pleasure?" My husband walks away, out of the store, and leaves me there, ducky in hand. At the counter I have extra money on my gift certificate so I grab a cock ring, *for him,* and throw it in.

Outside we look at each other, ready to explode, and then suddenly we both start laughing, like letting out air. The whole thing is absurd. This whole sex thing is out of control, it's so damn charged. Over the past three years, we've probably fought more about sex than had it. Where did the fun of it go? We've become so prickly since the baby. It's like we've taken every major issue—all the frustrations of adjusting to parenthood, all our household power struggles, our isolation, our personal demons, our fears about losing each other and losing ourselves—out on our poor sex life. Laughing it off for once really feels good—like a beginning, a much-needed do-over.

Over the past three years, we've probably fought more about sex **THAN HAD IT.**

"We need to eat," I say, and at the closest restaurant we order steak and eggs, and martinis that are so strong we leave them barely touched.

"Now what?" my husband asks as we finish. For a minute I try to read his mind, his signals, figure out what he's hoping I'll say. But that's the old us. That's the bad-sex kind of thinking; it's no longer the way to go. It's *for him* thinking, not *for me* thinking. I grab the keys and tell him, "It's a surprise."

By the time we get to the lake, clouds have come in; it's still warm but the air is wet, it feels like rain. At the canoe rental place my husband looks nervous, but game. "Put this on," I say, throwing him a life jacket as we put the boat in the water. We tip back and forth and splash trying to get into it, but soon, we're paddling away from shore, tilted, wobbly, imperfect. We paddle under the bridge and into tangles of green lily pads. My husband grins wildly; he's not a nature boy, he's a horrible swimmer, but I can tell he likes it out here. It's beautiful and quiet and just the two of us.

Within fifteen minutes, though, it starts pouring. We head toward the cover of trees on shore and pull our canoe up, laughing. "I want you," I say, and push him onto the wet grass. I pull his pants down and kiss him, then slide on the cock ring I've kept in my pocket. He's impressed. I get on top of him, my jeans around my ankles and rain pouring onto my face. From my position I can see the cars on the bridge, whizzing past. It makes me excited to think they might see us; they could if they just slowed down. I speed up. I can tell already that I'm not going to come; there's not enough room for me to squirm around on him, to get the friction I need for that to happen, but it's not bad sex. It's deep and fast, and without having to worry about coming I focus just on the other sensations that I'm experiencing: slippery, rough, warm, wet. We're connected, it's thrilling. This is the difference, I think, between true charity sex and a pity fuck. I'm not doing it for me, to relieve guilt or check it off a list. I'm doing for him, yes, but because I want to. Because I want to give him something of me, because I love him, because I'm turned on, because it's fun. We keep going until finally he pulls out and comes on my stomach, under the wet shirt he's hiked up over my breasts. We hear the crackling of branches and scramble to pull ourselves together, just in time; fellow canoers are seeking refuge in the trees nearby. We hold hands and sneak back to the canoe. Giggling as we put our life jackets on, we push off back into the rain, which has let up to a drizzle. We head back, soaking wet but happy; we're flushed and laughing and freezing. We turn in our canoe, and with time still to kill we drive to the hot tub place and get a room. "We got stuck in the rain," we mumble as the woman hands us towels and shows us our room. As if we need an excuse. "We need to warm up."

In our room we strip and put our clothes in the sauna to dry. With all the pressure of big-date sex out of the way, we sit in the hot tub and talk. I think about our time in the bushes—how hard he was for so long, how open and excited and happy he seemed, how my senses went into overdrive—and I scoot a little closer. His knee rubs between my legs, and suddenly I am on fire. The books, the rubber ducky, the steak for breakfast, our hot naked bodies—it's gotten me all worked up. I climb out of the tub and pull him out with me. I know what I want. I whisper in his ear exactly what I want him to do to me; I grab myself and show him, just in case he wasn't listening. Inside me, he's hard again, and I'm hungry; forget candy bars and babies and bartenders and smoking. I love the perfect way my husband and I fit, the way he so totally fills me up, the way he completes me, the way he feels like all that I need. I can't stand it, I can't stand it—it's too much. There's nothing I can do but let go and enjoy it, *for me.*

• • • • • • • • • • • • • •

Several weeks later I'm at the gym again with my daughter. I'm helping her shower and get dressed after her swim lesson so I can walk her down to the gym's childcare and leave her for an hour while I work on my own swimming. In the shower, my daughter shoves me off as I finger her hair. I leave her for a minute to use the bathroom. As I'm walking away, she cups her hand to her mouth—the wrong way—and shouts across the room: "*Mama, you goin' poop or pee?*" I cringe as the naked women around us laugh, and I quietly mouth back, "Pee." I close the door to the stall, then grin as I hear her yell again, as loud as she can, "*From your bagina?*"

As much as I'm embarrassed, I'm also proud. Her grandma would be, too. My little girl is carrying the family torch. She is sharp, outspoken, shameless. She knows how to speak up, she knows what she wants, and she's learning to use her own voice. She will make her own mistakes, but she also knows I'm there to shout to, to cry on, to help put the pieces together when she needs me to—just like I'm trying to do in my own life now. Fired up in my own way by her young confidence, I yell back, liltlessly: "Yep, my vagina."

Freedom, Baby

CHAPTER 7

Sexual liberation is one aspect of personal liberation.

—LONNIE BARBACH, PhD, *For Yourself: The Fulfillment of Female Sexuality*

Between my sister-in-law, the swim instructor, and now my mom, who has promised to come up from California and do it with me, I'm pretty much committed to this triathlon thing. I've started working out with one of my girlfriends. We call it our "Fit and Fabulous" program, though most days we're more like "Fat and Fibulous," opting for the executive workout instead: We sit on our butts in the steam room bitching and dishing. I complain about JB's selective senses (sight, smell) when it comes to housework and how his family calls me directly when they want to talk because they know he's phone-challenged and can't manage to return a call. My girlfriend tells me about her late-night booty call from an ex-boyfriend, her current proclivity for young Russian men, and the cute paramedic who saved her neighbor's life. As much as I hate to admit it, exercise is doing me right. Even upping it just a small amount has brought noticeable benefits: My blood is pumping, flowing through my veins, engorging walls in all the right spots, and carrying whispers of something that feels a lot like life.

With my hormones mellowing out, things are taking on a new equilibrium. My daughter and I have a new rhythm. We're no longer wrestling as much as dancing; we still step on each other's toes, but we're quicker to get back on track, to reconnect. We've both grown so much over the past couple of months; I can see now that I don't have to depend on her to make my life whole. It's not her job to keep me in line or in the safety of sweatpants.

While I'm starting to fill some of the holes opened up by my daughter's independence with my own, I'm filling others of them with my husband. We have a new rhythm, too. We even signed up for a weekly tango class, determined to move out of our boring rut. Of course, we got lost on the way to our first class, fought the whole time about how I didn't let him lead, and eventually gave up on it altogether, using the time instead to get burgers, or pop into an old dive bar, or check out some music. But at least we're doing things—we have new energy to put into our relationship and each other. And it's paying off with wonderful side effects; I'm finding that we're having a sexual renaissance. All of a sudden sex is at the top of our list; finally it's something we talk about, a lot, right along with "What's on TV?" and "Pass the salsa." Formerly innocent situations take on a naughty angle: Picking up new shelves at IKEA, with our daughter in the children's playroom, we eye the practically abandoned restrooms. *Could we? Would we? Should we?* We don't, but shopping is so much more fun with that question in the air. Shopping is so much more fun when my husband grabs my hand and kisses it, for no reason at all.

Between writing my column, reading every sex book I can get my hands on, and researching the topic on my own (thumbs up on that rubber ducky, by the way), I've gotten back to enjoying sex; it has become, amazingly enough, something that no longer causes epic battles. Because we're having enough of it, and talking sanely enough about it when we don't, it has become a non-issue. Turning sex into a project, an ongoing discussion between us, has taken the tension and charge out it, but not the thrill. Which makes it much more appealing. We're still not getting busy with anywhere near the frequency we once did, but it doesn't matter. The sex we are having is so good that how often it happens is a moot point. When we connect, we connect; often, it's a two- or three-part event. Enough juices are finally flowing to recharge us, keeping us flush even in case of a drought. We're not in a state of panic about sex anymore; my husband knows it will happen eventually, and I've learned that saying no to him isn't the end of the world, or the end of true love. It's a good combination we've got going: the excitement of rediscovering each other and the comfort of communicating about what we really want.

I'm finding that I like sex harder and deeper than I did before. Of course, it is harder (at least to make time for) and deeper (metaphysically speaking). My body is changing, too. As I get to know my cycle again, post-breastfeeding, I'm noticing how my sex drive comes and goes with it. When my libido's here, it's much stronger than it was pre-baby. At the right time of the month, all it takes to get me going is to think of a certain position or one of my latest imaginary hot encounters (there's a cute young checker at Whole Foods). Now that I'm getting back in touch with myself so much (pun intended), I can actually feel myself ovulating; it's like a miniperiod in the middle of my cycle. At these times I gush in ways I never gushed, and I literally ache to get pregnant again; my biological clock goes off with the force of a steam engine. *All babies aboard! Last stop on the baby train!*

Freedom, Baby

I remember I was in my late teens, dating guys who were (clearly) in their sexual peak, the early twenties, when I first heard that a woman's sexual peak happens in her early thirties. At the time I imagined my early-thirties self: a professional psychologist in a cute business suit, with a bunch of young twenty-something playboys keeping me company. When the reality of my thirties hit—*Here I am, ready to peak . . . Can we get a peak here? Um, hello?*—I was totally perplexed. Then, later, I got mad. Why would nature play such a cruel joke on us anyway? Making us "peak" when we're making babies and could care less?

But now, I can see it. It's just different than I thought. I still don't think about sex as often as a young twentysomething playboy would, but when I do, it's with a new intensity. And when we get around to it, it's definitely *right.* It's ravenous and more than a little risky. I get impatient with condoms, and want to take my husband inside me a second time, and a third. I want to throw my birth control caution to the wind and use him over and over again.

But I don't. Because the rest of the month I really don't want a new baby. It's not just the prospect of reacquainting myself with unrelenting morning (ha! Try twenty-four hour!) sickness, or having another uncomfortable pregnancy, that gets me. It's not those early days of poop, puke, and deprivation that turn me off, or the sketchy division of labor (both kinds—childbirth *and* housework), or the fact that I am finally beginning to recognize my husband again, beginning to enjoy a new vocabulary that includes words like *playdate* and *quiet time*—and soon, we hope, the pie in the sky, the big romance: *sleepover.*

No. What *really* gets me about the idea of having more babies is the oppressive nature of fresh mother-love. It sneaks up so sweetly and then burrows itself into every part of me; it's like a life sentence with no time off for good (or, more importantly, bad) behavior, no sick days, and no easy outs. It's the kind of love that can make even the most devoted mommy fantasize about getting into her station wagon and going and going and never coming back, just to make sure she could. Just to make sure she was still herself.

* * *

"Go! Go! Go!" my husband commands, pushing me out the door. "You're going to be late!" It's true, I am—but I'm also in a fuddle about what to wear to the soccer game he has pushed me into—friends of his coffee-shop friends who play casually each Sunday.

"Why am I even going?" I play-pout, nervous and giddy about this new solo adventure, about being one of a couple women playing with a group of men I have never met. "Forget it," I say, "I haven't played in like a hundred years. I'm not going."

Freedom, Baby

"You're going," my husband says, walking me to the car and giving me a kiss, "because you love soccer."

Correction. I *loved* soccer, once, a long time ago. Back before I discovered boys and makeup and the thrill of sneaking cigarettes in dark alleys. Back before I threw myself into one-night stands and other people and true love. Back before my own desires were buried under a layer of steely mother-bliss. But now that it's time to start digging, I realize I've been hunting down more than just my missing libido. I've also been hunting down the missing *me*.

When I get to the field, I don't recognize anyone. I'm tempted to turn and flee to the safety of home, but soon I'm spotted by one of my husband's friends. She waves me over to a small group of guys kicking a ball around. I feel like I'm crashing a party; they're all friends, they're all artists, they're cool people with lots to say about their busy lives. I get insecure about my own life, as well as my soccer skills; I haven't played since before I started high school. And those executive workouts haven't exactly gotten me into the best shape.

Before long, we start to play. It's a close, friendly, sweaty game with no real rules, no referees, no attitude. I may be out of shape, but I find I still know how to move, I still have instincts, I'm still fast. Here on the soccer field, my body remembers: movement, sensation, the clarity of adrenaline. I can't remember the last time I really ran, for fun. I'm not jogging, or chasing a runaway toddler; I'm *running*, as fast and hard as I can.

After the first hour, we're joined by a group of young Argentineans. They're cute and generous with the ball; they're also very good, keeping the game fun and lively, showing off, bringing things up a notch. We keep playing. My legs are shaky, my muscles exhausted. I tell myself to slow down, take it easy, but I don't—I can't. I don't want to. Here, I am free, I have a pulse. Here, I'm alive. By the time the game is over I'm hot and sweat-soaked and, I admit, a little bit on fire. In the last two hours I have touched more men than I have in the past ten years. The smell of grass and dirt goes straight to the happy-memories part of my brain. The smell of my own sweat mixing with distinctly male sweat goes somewhere else entirely. It makes me remember the smell of my husband on one of our first dates: He came straight from moving furniture and met me for a picnic in the park. We lay on top of each other on a blanket and watched Opera in the Park—well, listened, really, because we were so busy making out

In the last two hours, I have touched more men than I have in the **PAST TEN YEARS.**

and trying to touch each other without being seen. He smelled like sweat and the sex we would have that night when we got home—and in the morning, and the next night. He smelled to me like lust, like falling in love.

Miraculously, I get home from soccer to find a quiet, relatively clean house. While my daughter naps my husband draws me a bath and sits at the edge of the tub as I show off my new scrapes, my new good mood. He feigns jealousy as I tell him about the unexpected body-bumping bonuses of coed soccer. I watch as he watches me in the tub, his body showing the effects of my nakedness.

Finishing up, still overheated and exhausted, I get out and flop on the bed. For the first time in a long time my body is tired in a good way, from exercise rather than sleep deprivation or stress. My husband lays his head on my belly and runs his hand up my leg, feeling out where I'm at, trying to see if I'm in the mood. I am. "You just lie there," he says, scooting down to kiss me, letting out hot breath where I'm already plenty hot. "You rest and let me take care of everything else." And I do.

With all the excitement my husband comes quickly, pulling out just in time—a dangerous game I've realized I don't want to play anymore. With all this sex and new freedom, maybe it's time to look into a more permanent form of birth control; there are some things that are easier for me to do with one kid, easier to do if I don't find myself pregnant again just yet. Things I'd forgotten once mattered to me, like soccer, and sex, and having a life.

* * *

What's that saying? *Want to make God laugh? Tell him your plans.*

Just like that, literally overnight, we've become a two-kid family—something I once thought I wanted, until, of course, it actually happened. With his brother in trouble with the law again, my husband's seven-year-old niece, Nicky, has come to stay with us, indefinitely, carrying a giant duffel bag of ill-fitting clothes that smell like cats and cigarette smoke. For a week, we all sneeze, even the dogs. Unexpectedly, I am delightfully busy—and loving it. Our house is a crazy, upside-down mess of girl mania: art supplies, horses, and all things pink, purple, and Polly Pocket. Our male dog hides downstairs; my husband suggests we hire a housecleaner. For some ungodly reason I say, "I think I can handle it."

I like the idea of handling it. I like the way another kid puts my own life on hold again; I like the way "Let's go, girls!" rolls off my tongue at the zoo, so expertly controlled and pointed. I like being part of that strangely relaxed two-kid crowd (*Oh, they're around here somewhere . . .*). I even like the way at the end of the day I feel I've earned the right to watch three hours of crap on TV—I'm too tired to read, to think, to write, to share. Two kids, I've learned quickly, means more than twice as much housework, less than half as much sex, and, like, five times as much driving.

Not unlike the very first weeks with our daughter, Nicky's arrival spurs my husband and me to become a fine-tuned kid-rearing machine again. We take turns, pass off, and finally lie together tenderly on the couch and share bedtime battle stories. We're drawn closer by our mutual responsibility. We don't have sex, but we don't fight about it, either. We don't fight about anything; we're too tired.

Despite the closeness we have at first, I soon feel my husband starting to slip again. Concern for his brother, Nicky's dad, brings him back to the kind of worrying he was doing when we first met, the kind of worrying he's been doing on some level for his whole life. He's afraid his brother is back on a slippery slope of depression and drug use, slipping into trouble he might not make it out of. So my husband does what I've long since discovered that he does when he has strong feelings: He shuts down. He spends more time sleeping, more time spacing out, and more time pulling into himself than he spends pulling his weight around the house. And so I do what I've always done in response: I freak out, panic that I'm losing him, and try to yell him back to me. And then I act, I control. I clean, I cook, I shuttle. I put the girls on a strict schedule for my own sanity's sake: activity, quiet time, playtime, dinnertime, bedtime. No *if*s or *but*s allowed. I over-parent, over-housewife, and overreact to every situation JB withdraws from. His depression is like an energy vortex in our house, sucking away our closeness, warping our sexual upswing. I try to explain to him why his disconnectedness is so hard to live with, but he doesn't get it. He's got a job, he's not on drugs, he's not in jail, he's not cheating on me; that's success, in his family. That should be enough. What's the big deal with a little depression? So what if he's a zombie now and then? But it is a big deal for me. I feel like I have three kids to take care of now, not two.

It's those early days with my daughter all over again; I feel overwhelmed and alone. I know I could reach out to JB with sex; physical connection tethers him to this world in the same way emotional connection does for me. I know there are things he can say to me and show me with his body that he can't with words, but it's hard for me to reach out when I feel so far away. It's hard to put out an olive branch when I'm tired and resentful and would rather stick it in his eye, just to make sure he can feel *something.* The fact that we've been here before and survived it should be a comfort, but it's not. I hate the chaos of change, and I hate it even more when I feel like he's not really there to help me with it, when it feels like he can't even see me. It's frustrating; just when I've started to figure things out, there's a new bump. We were just so close, and now we're on other planets again.

Tired of the view from across the universe, I spend more and more time playing soccer. I line up playdates like crazy for the girls, then force JB to be on top of things by leaving him to drive and pick up and be in charge while I escape the chaos of our house. I go to the field early to run laps or stay out late after soccer getting beers or lie in the late-afternoon sun while the Argentineans smoke pot and pass around a wine bottle of maté. Sunday after Sunday, I call my husband and tell him the game went late again; I'll be home soon, order pizza again.

They can't make me go back, I think. But of course, I do. It strikes me as another irony of motherhood that we arrive here via that essential and inalienable human right, freedom of choice. Because mother-love is the anti-freedom, the anti-choice. There's no escaping it; of course I could run, but I wouldn't really be free. I'd always feel the tug, and be pulled home.

At Target I pick up some hip-hugging sweatpants and a tight white shirt. I shave my armpits. I start wearing sweatproof makeup. I'm obsessed with Sundays; I'm a soccer stalker. It's all I think about, all I want. It is a tiny oasis for me, a place where I can hide and escape and find myself again after a long week of giving too much. It's also a place brimming with adult energy—and it's a place where somebody grown-up notices me.

The next Sunday, at soccer, I'm sprinting to beat my favorite twenty-two-year-old Argentinean to the ball. We get there at the same time and crash into each other, our heat and breath and sweat mingling as we fall, arms and legs colliding into each other.

"Sorry! Sorry!" he shouts, jumping up and offering me his hand. I take it. The feeling is electric. His youth, his energy, and his thinly veiled attraction to me are heart-stopping—and a huge turn-on. I freeze and for a moment envision our life together: freedom in the Argentinean heat, no kids, no husband, no details. We roll in warm rain, our skin like fire, consuming. He is wild and relentless. We spend hours sipping maté and reading poetry. He sings a song in my ear; I inhale his youth, get lost, forget.

"Need a lift home?" I ask him after the game, knowing full well he does; he does every week. He climbs in, smiling. His short shaved hair looks like my husband's did ten years ago when we met. I lose a breath remembering how it felt to rub my hands so close to my husband's skull, how I'd rub his head as his body shook and he came all over me. By now I know the way to the Argentinean's house. I also know his name, what he does, and how to flirt shamelessly with him under the guise of playing soccer. I know how it feels when he puts his hand on my lower back, laughing as he tries to get the ball, grabbing my waist as he spins around me. We sit in front of his house making small talk; the sexual tension is almost unbearable. I want to jump on top of him, attack him, suck the youth and sex and energy out of him like an aging vampire. I want to lick the sweat off his pretty face, give myself over to him. I want to show him what my body can really do, off the field, in private, in his messy twenty-two-year-old's room. "Do you want to come in for a beer?" he asks, using his accent to let me in on all the possibilities, to make it nearly impossible to say no.

We sit in front of his house making small talk; the sexual tension is **ALMOST UNBEARABLE.**

I do say no, though. I say no and give a casual wave and smile as I get the hell out of there. When I'm safely blocks away, I pull over and start to cry—not just from guilt over what I almost did, but out of sadness over what I didn't do, over what officially I'm never supposed to do again. I miss that thrill so much, that electricity, that rush of new lust. But it's really something more that I miss. I miss the freedom of acting on instinct—of not having to think everything through, of not caring so damn much, of not having anything to lose.

Two weeks earlier I completed my triathlon, squeaking by my goal with three minutes to spare. It was scary and thrilling; my buried competitive side pushed me until I thought I might drown, or pass out, or just sit down and start crying at the emotional sight of so many women pushing themselves, pushing their bodies so hard. As I started the final leg, the three-mile run, I was shaky and unsure, until I heard people yelling my name from the sidelines. When I turned around, dazed, I saw my husband and the girls right in front, jumping up and down, beaming and waving. My daughter ran out onto the course, grabbing and hugging my leg, kissing it madly. “Go Mama! Go!” she cheered, and ran back to the side. I blew them all kisses and kept going, energized by their belief in me.

This is the thing: I do have something to lose now. I have a lot to lose. Yes, domestic life is horribly boring at times. Yes, I’m married to an on-again, off-again mental zombie. Yes, motherlove can be as disorienting as vertigo. But these things aren’t static. They’re like my libido: they ebb and flow, they’re here, they’re there, they’re gone, then back again, better than ever, and then, in a moment, gone again. It’s true that we’re no longer who we were before, but we also won’t be who we are now forever. We’re always moving in an orbital dalliance, JB and I; we’re two separate planets each on our own elliptical path, passing close in conjunction, nearly invisible in opposition. But we never stop moving. And we never stop feeling the pull of the other, reminding us to stay in this world, reminding us we're not alone in the universe. And to me, that seems worth holding on to.

At the end of the summer Nicky leaves nearly as suddenly as she came, off to stay with other aunts and uncles on her mom's side of the family. We're all sad, and, I confess, a little relieved. Our house feels empty and ghostly quiet. My daughter plays quietly by herself for hours on end; we all need some time alone. Anxious to reconnect, to bring my husband back to me, I suggest we finally use the gift certificate we have to a hot springs resort in Canada. *Take a weekend away from the kids every three months*—another prescription from the magazines for rekindling romance. That night we sit on the porch drinking wine and try to hammer down the childcare details. I'm really nervous about leaving my daughter; since her birth, three years ago, I have not spent one night away from her. I figure out that for over one thousand nights, I've slept with her within arm's reach. When I tell my husband that, he's as surprised as I am at the number, and suddenly he has another idea. "Why don't you just go alone? For you?" This, from the guy who has spent the past three years trying to get me alone in a hotel room. It's so sweet that he would want this for me. It's a purely unselfish gift I wouldn't have even known I wanted. I know that despite his zombification he was touched by the way I was with Nicky, the way I consider his family—and all their drama—mine, without any question. I know he saw how much more work I took on with another child around, how hard it was. But I also think he's finally getting something we both need to learn: You can't give yourself freely to others if you're not whole yourself. There's too much at stake, too much to lose.

In those early years together, filling each other's empty spaces was enough for us. It wasn't all just chemical lust that made us so sexually charged; in some ways I think we actually thought we could fuck each other into being less broken, into being whole. And for a little while I think it worked, until we became parents and a whole new depth opened in our lives, a whole new concept of what "whole" might mean.

The night before I leave for my one-night, two-day trip away, my husband and I make love on the couch after watching a chick flick together, a post-bedtime video date, complete with popcorn and hand-holding. We start off slowly, quietly, the deep kind of connected sex where we're as close as two people can be; our eyes are open, we're communicating, we're saying: *Slow and easy feels pretty damn good. Comfortable feels good.* We get louder, we get faster; we're all over the couch, onto the floor, against the wall. And then our eyes are closed; we're two kids again, taking what we need, pounding out our flaws and broken pieces; we're carnal, we're insatiable, we're really, really hot. This is something else worth holding on to—the Supermom of sex lives. We've come to a place where we can have it all, where we can let go and be as naughty as we want to be, or as safe.

On the three-hour drive up to the hot springs the next day, I keep checking the rearview mirror; it's odd to drive with no one sitting in back. As I cross the border into Canada, my stomach flips. I'm out of mother-wife jurisdiction now, in another country. I could just keep going, become an international family fugitive. I stick to my MapQuest directions, though, following winding highways through the giant green spaces and shades of Northwest gray I grew up with. I think back to my very first trip to San Francisco, the way I threw everything I owned into my little Honda Civic and just started driving. I remember my first road trip back to visit, too—how I headed north after spending the night with a boyfriend, how I left early in the morning with a hangover from hell and his advice to keep awake by playing with myself. "That's what I would do," he grumbled as I kissed his cheek and left. I took his advice, blatantly doing it as I passed a big rig truck, slowing for a view, then speeding up and off and away. Naughty me now is not so different, just a lot safer.

I check into the hotel, get settled in my room, and spend the rest of the day in water. Hot water, cold water, tepid and steamed. The minerals from the natural springs make me buoyant. I backfloat in the cool outdoor pool and stare at the dark gray sky and a giant evergreen. It feels right to be here. Not just here, today, by myself, but here, in the Northwest, living in Seattle, back home. In my room I rest, then get dressed and head to the restaurant for the prime rib buffet dinner. "Will anyone be joining you?" the waitress asks. I shake my head, but I'm tempted to tell her about my husband and daughter, as if I need an excuse. I order a glass of wine and head to the buffet. "What piece would you like?" a white-aproned young man says from behind the platter of meat. *You'll do,* I think, and blush imagining having the nerve to slip him my room number. I smile and point to the piece I'd like, then go back to the table and drink my wine. I worry for a minute that all my searching for my lost

I worry for a minute that all my searching for my lost libido has turned me into a **SEX MONSTER.**

libido (and maybe, just maybe, getting closer to finding it) has turned me into a sex monster. But I know I won't really be slipping anyone any numbers; I'm just playing naughty, because I can. I busy myself with my meat and with flirting with the baby at the table next to me. While I'm eating, it occurs to me that many of the sexually successful dates JB and I have had in the past three years have had meat on the menu. Maybe it's that simple. Maybe that's the true key to finding my lost libido—eating more meat.

After dinner I soak some more, then head inside and off to my appointment for a sea-salt scrub. The scrubbing isn't so rough it hurts, but it's close. The woman's allegiance is clearly to my skin; she disregards my nakedness, scrubbing between my upper thighs and under my breasts like I'm nothing but a body, then pulling me and turning me to get each nook and cranny. Each time she takes the warm bucket of water and flushes it over me, I relax more. I feel myself opening up, layers of dead skin, dead me, washing off and going down the drain. After a gentle massage, she squirts warm lotion up and down my body, working it slowly into each body part. With my eyes closed, I feel like a baby; I'm new, I'm cared for, I'm just born. By the time I get back to my room, it's late. I call my husband to check in but no one answers. I try to worry, but I'm too relaxed. I flip on the TV and watch a sex-positive porn station (Oh, Canada!) and drift off imagining the things I would do to my husband in this room, the things I'll do when we do come here, just the two of us.

The next day, after spending the morning in the pools again, I check out. I'm floating. With the room, the scrub, and the prime rib dinner I still get $1.75 back from the gift certificate, originally meant for both of us. Before I leave, I take a walk through the woods—it's just about to rain, it's dark and wet and cold. All alone with the trees and wilderness I grew up with, I think I hear someone or something calling me, and I strain to listen. "I'm here," I say out loud. "I'm listening." But there's no answer. There's just a kind of quiet inside me that I haven't felt before. I take a deep breath and try to remember this moment, this feeling of being alone, alive, and connected to something larger.

On the way home I'm sure I'm going to die. It's pouring fat rain and dark; the road is slippery and hard to see. I curse our car, our very not-soccer-mom bright green sedan, as I hydroplane on a puddle. I slip around, then finally slow down and get back in control. *Fuck this,* I think. *I'm getting that damn SUV.* I guess I don't mind being a soccer mom so much now anyway, especially since I am, in the truest sense, a soccer mom. When I finally get home, safe and sound, I feel like I've been gone for a year. In all my fresh, quiet clarity I make another decision, too. I'm finally going to make that appointment to get an IUD. I'm ready to buy myself a little more freedom—freedom from condoms, freedom to be spontaneous again, and, most importantly, freedom to explore these new parts of myself and my relationship before throwing another baby into the mix.

A couple weeks later I show up to my ob-gyn's office in my new low-mileage Subaru Forester (very fancy, but not too horribly suburban—I like to think, at least). I've got an appointment to get an IUD inserted, but it turns out my doctor is out delivering a baby. I opt to stick with my appointment by using the on-call doctor and take it as a good sign when she introduces herself as—no joke—*Dr. Freely.* As in, you can have sex *freely* now. As in, you can work on that life of yours *freely* now. As in, you are now free to move about the cabin and condom-*freely* become a member of the mile-high club!

While Dr. Freely preps me, I lie back on the exam table and study the butterfly mobile hanging from the ceiling. I cramp as she inserts a copper IUD into my uterus. The butterflies blur with the sharp, searing pain, and I realize I am crying. I cry for all the sterile ceilings I have stared up at in my life: my first trip to Planned Parenthood; an abortion when I was nineteen; the birth of my daughter. I cry for my great-grandmother who died from a botched abortion, leaving nine young children motherless. I cry because I will most likely never be pregnant by accident again, maybe never even pregnant again. I cry because I can feel history in the making. I can feel the power this choice holds, the weight of this gift, the choices I have now that my own mother and grandmother and great-grandmother did not.

I hug Dr. Freely on the way out, pick up my daughter from preschool, and float, unsettled and giddy, through the day, much as I did when I first discovered I was pregnant with Ramona—*my* little secret inside me, *my* life, *my* dreams.

That night, I dream the boys from soccer have invited me to join them as traveling gypsies in faraway places. In my dream I am thrilled, vibrant, flirtatious. It is not until I am actually at the airport that it hits me—in the same shocking dream-way you realize you've shown up to school naked—that I could never go. That I have a daughter, a husband, a family, a life. It's not always naughty, it's not always easy, it's not always fun. But somehow, it's always worth it. I wake up as my daughter climbs into bed with us and I pull her close; my husband loops an arm around us both. Sometimes, I'm learning, you don't have to run to be free. Sometimes it's all right here.

It's not always naughty, it's not always easy, it's not always fun. But somehow,

IT'S ALWAYS WORTH IT.

AFTERGLOW

THREE YEARS–PRESENT

Epilogue

Just Do It

Awake is the new sleep
Awake is the new sleep
So wake up, and do it
Whatever it is
Just do it

—BEN LEE

Having good sex with someone is like learning how to ride a bike. You never really forget how, but it's easy to get out of practice; and getting back on can leave you feeling a little sore. The payoff, though, is huge. In no time you're flying, cruising along: *Look, Ma, no hands!* Four and a half years after our sex life was thrown into chaos, we're back on the bike, full speed ahead. Our sex life is better than ever; it's wild, it's tame, it's naughty; it may go on vacation from time to time but it's always *there,* in one way or another. That doesn't mean it's perfect; with our busy, child-filled lives we still often end up Sexless in Seattle, but I guess through this whole journey, this case, this mystery of the missing libido, I found what I was looking for—a way to be the best mommy I can be, while still being naughty, while still being me.

While it's true that I do see a lot more of my libido lately, it's still quite independent and very catlike, showing up out of the blue, seemingly disinterested but meowing and demanding attention, then just as quickly and quietly sneaking off again. I have come to see it as my picky, fickle companion. I have also come to realize how complicated and multilayered it is. Recently, I got my testosterone level checked, just to see if that was playing a role in my naughty ups and downs. But I landed right in the middle: perfectly average, perfectly acceptable. I think a part of me was hoping the test would show something else, something purely biological that would offer me an easy fix, a way to always feel naughty, a way to always be able to match my husband. I continue to be floored by the complexities involved in turning a woman on—in what it takes to get me going. I'm fascinated by how much of it is cyclical, how much mental, how much emotional, how much physical. I know that I'll never pin it all down, but I'm certainly getting closer. I know now that those first couple years of motherhood can really take their toll. I also know that if there's anything big going on in my life, my libido is one of the first things to go; a little bit of stress and it runs for the hills. Case in point: As I finish up this book I confess to logging a pitiful number of miles on my IUD. But last month we gave 'er a run for the money; last month we were so busy conducting book "research" we had a sex surplus.

This is probably the biggest change in our sex life: We're relaxed about it. That's not to say we're lazy or neglectful; sex is now a much bigger priority to both of us than it was before.

But we're also not on edge about it all the time. We know we'll get around to it eventually, and we're not panicked that if we miss a week, or even two, it means we're getting divorced, or falling out of love. It usually just means we're busy. JB sums it up so well: "Sex used to take about as much effort and planning as cracking open an after-work beer. Sometimes it was flat, sometimes it exploded all over. But there were always five more in the fridge. Now, sex is more like a weekly bottle of expensive champagne instead of a daily pint, but who's complaining?"

Now, sex is more like a weekly bottle of EXPENSIVE CHAMPAGNE *instead of a daily pint.*

Just Do It

It's true that our sex life now may not have all the energy and desperation of those early years together (although, then again, neither do we), but it still rocks our domestic little world in a whole new way; *game on.* Now, we try new things, and we do the same old thing, and they're both pretty damn good. Now, we don't force naughtiness; we're not counting, we're not comparing, we're not competing. We're just doing it, for us, for each other, for fun.

We've also learned how good it can feel to let go. Before, our fights would turn into giant tug-of-wars, each of us stuck on an end, afraid to budge, afraid to give an inch. But it only takes one person to drop the rope. It doesn't take much to give in. Sometimes, you just have to do it.

Sex, I've found, is like that too. Sometimes I don't think I want it, but if I *just do it,* just make time for it, I find I actually like it, a lot. It used to be I'd try to do it for him, but now I try doing it for me. I'm not giving away something I resent; I'm treating myself to what I know I need—even when I don't know I need it. And the more I like it, the more I want it. Sex has become the new foreplay for me; it loosens me up, juices me up, brings us together. With the IUD, I can take advantage of this. With my husband's needs out of the way, I focus on my own; I'm excited, and I can take my time. It's a good match; no matter how satisfied my husband is, he always has time for round two, or three if we're lucky. Just doing it in this way isn't the same as having bad sex; there's no resentment in it, no lack of communication, and no one is being or feeling used. Sometimes just doing it means just saying no; sometimes it means *I just need some space.* Sometimes it means *Go ahead, take a chance, it might be great.* But now it almost always means real connection. We've stopped second-guessing each other, or just plain old guessing what the other person wanted, and started asking, *Do you like that? Do you want that? Do you want to try this?* It doesn't take away the magic or the romance; it makes sex more exciting.

And finding excitement in domestic life is certainly a challenge. Watching *Beauty and the Beast* for the thousandth time makes you start hearing the song lyrics differently, just to keep yourself amused: "*Tale as old as time, quaaludes and red wine . . . Beauty and the Beast.*" With us both working at home, it's still easy to get too comfortable, but we're committed to finding the naughty moments whenever we can; we make dates, take advantage of any alone time, and save energy and water by showering together. Recently, while our daughter took a rare late nap upstairs, I snuck into the shower with my husband. Over the sounds of the water and our making out, I kept thinking I heard her crying. "Just relax," my husband said, lathering soap up and down my back, pressing me against the cool glass door. "She's four years old. If she wakes up she can come downstairs and knock on the door." I was tempted to flip my switch back to "Mommy" and run up and check on her, but my body was saying something else. My body was saying, *Let go, she's fine, you need this.* She was fine, and I did need it. Maybe now, so many years after buying it, we're finally ready to use that super-duper baby monitor.

For me, motherhood was so consuming because I couldn't treat it like a side dish; it felt so all-or-nothing. Over the years, though, I learned that it's less all-or-nothing than it is a fine balancing act—of knowing when to hold on to myself, my daughter, my marriage; and knowing when to let go of fear, of society's fucked-up ideas, of my daughter, of old baggage. Good sex, I think, takes a lot of these same skills, too. It involves learning to hold on to yourself in a relationship, to what you have together, to the moment. And it also takes letting go of great sexpectations, of puritan hang-ups, of resentments, of everything but *right here, right now.*

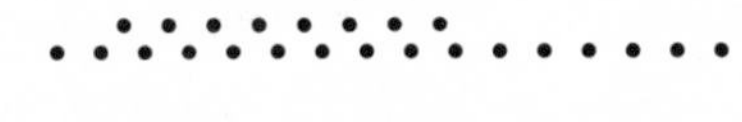

Sex in marriage *isn't something to take or leave . . . it holds us together and fills us up the way nothing else can.*

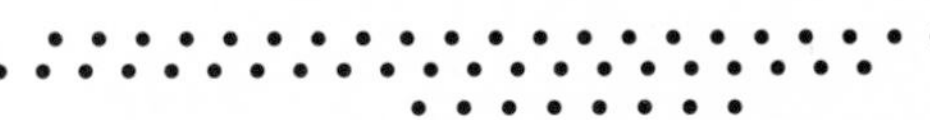

It's much more natural for me to relegate sex to side-dish status, but I don't think it belongs there any more than motherhood does. Sex in marriage isn't something to take or leave. It's the staple, the glue; it's sticky and messy, and it holds us together and fills us up in a way nothing else can. And while both being a mother and a sexual person can be like trying to consume two big, heavy entrées, sometimes it's better to be a little overfull than still hungry, still wanting.

The past four years have been a crazy roller coaster ride. But through it, I've realized that the process of finding and holding on to my libido is a lot like the actual act of sex. It's about the journey, not the destination. It's about finding a way to be in my body, in the moment. It's about being aware of my feelings, focusing on myself, being open to another person. Every time I got caught up thinking, *Where is this going? What if I don't find it? What's wrong with me?* I took a step back, a step away from getting there. Like sex, coming into motherhood and myself and my libido has been all about learning how to hold on and how to let go. It's been about figuring out how to hang on to myself after motherhood, how to hold on to my relationship and my dreams and my desires and needs when I'm so beautifully and exhaustedly consumed by a tiny other. It's about letting go of the outdated idea that a happily-ever-after might come without ever having to really work for it.

Sex, for us, is about taking the time to really see each other—the *us* buried under "mom" and "dad," "husband" and "wife." It's about growing up, waking up, and making new promises to each other all the time: *I promise to let you grow, I promise to still have fun, I promise to be careful with crushes and drinking and dancing when I'm not with you.* It *is* dangerous to have a life and be married. You run into people and situations that can throw things upside down. It's easier to be safe when you're not all *Footloose* about life. But it's even more dangerous, I think, to give up being true to your life and having fun because you're scared. It's worse, I think, to slowly fade away into quiet comfort and pretend you never really cared about being together or being fully alive.

We went out to dinner with friends recently: a couple with a one-year-old, and a newlywed friend visiting from out of town. (She is, in fact, the former girlfriend JB left for me, so long ago.) After getting the rundown on her wedding and the good gossip on old friends, I asked if she wanted to have kids. "Well, *I* do," she said, "but I'm not so sure my husband wants to. He has this idea that when you have kids, your life is, like, over or something." She laughed and then paused. "But it's not, right?"

The four of us parents just kind of smiled and nodded noncommittally, in that tired noncommittal parental way we practice for things like invitations to events that last past ten. No. Life is definitely not over. Life is even more lifelike than ever before. It's more of everything: more fun, more feeling, more worries, more exhaustion. Life is not over. But life as you knew it *before*, that probably is. It's yet another thing to let go of, while holding on to what you are now, what you have now. Because *now* is really where it's at.

Recently, my husband and I were in Hawaii again, this time for my mom's wedding. It was inspiring to see her let go of her old fears and affirm what she and her partner have together. She's taking a leap, opening herself up, and doing it with her eyes wide open. My daughter and I got to Hawaii three weeks before JB arrived, to spend time with my family. She and I spent long lazy days together, like we did when she was a baby. It was just the two of us again: snuggling in the sun, building sand castles, swimming with the turtles, floating on our backs. The night before JB came into town, my mom offered to take Ramona out for a couple hours the next day so he and I could "make love" (again, *Ew, Mom!*) after being apart for so long. Even my brother joked that maybe I should go pick JB up from the airport alone and just head straight to our hotel room. (This is what happens when you start writing about sex. . . .) The funny thing, though, is that JB and I weren't worried about that at all. We were hungry for each other, and excited and giddy after being apart for so long, but we weren't frantic for sex. We knew that eventually we'd carve out some time alone together; we knew there was always a bed or a nap or a long shower that would bring us back together. We knew, without a doubt, we'd get our reunion sex. This is us now: patient, controlled, deep. We trust each other, we trust our relationship, we see the big picture without getting lazy.

By the time we had our alone time it was what we knew it would be. It was motel sex and Mexico sex and hot tub sex all rolled into one. It was old-days sex, and new-days sex, and what's-still-to-come sex, on the floor and the bed and the balcony, in the hot, wet air filled with the smell of plumeria and, of course, each other.

Magic *is* alive, and so, still, are we.

Just Us Always

Amare quello che desidero
Desidero la quale amoro
(To love the one you desire
to desire the one you love)

—JB BERNASKI

Before we were a family there was just us. Just you and me. It was even documented on a cheesy mirror we found in a gas station just outside of Reno: Just Us Always, *it said in fat red script with hearts and roses like the ones found in the package of rub-on tattoos our daughter now loves so much.*

Before you were the father of my child, you were my husband, my best friend, my keeper of secrets. Here's to going backward, to finding ourselves, to always having Reno. Here's to us, Husband.

Just Us Always

Here are my confessions.

I miss the way we were. I miss you and me and motel rooms. Hotel rooms. Sleazy, smoke-encrusted, dressed up, dark, hot, air-conditioned, middle of the road, four star, no star, cold tight sheets, ice machines, tiptoes, empty, used, just used rooms. The anonymity of them. The proximity of them—to each other, to naughtiness, to mystery, freedom. To fantasy.

I miss the jingle of the key, or the card, that lets you in. The newly dried shower, the minibar, the bottle of booze, the plastic tumblers. I miss the ashtrays. The lack of clutter. The thick shades. The unfiltered light. The discolorations. The late-night TV. The sex channels. The giant, firm, center-of-the-whole-room, center-of-the-whole-world bed.

I miss sitting at a Formica vanity, putting on makeup, pulling up stockings. I miss crotchless panties, legs spread just enough at the hotel bar. I miss sitting there, pretending. Pretending I'm alone. Pretending you're not looking at me. Pretending I don't know you. I miss taking you home, like a stranger, to a strange room. I miss the feel of ripping fishnet, breaking like spiderweb against my thighs as you take what you need, hungry, mysterious, and anonymous. Never mind that the credit card has both our names on it. Never mind that you'd punch the lights out of anyone else caught looking.

I love the way we are. I love the gray taking over your beard. I love your belly, all full and content. I love being the wife of the sexy devoted-dad guy the girls at the coffee shop all have the hots for. I love that you make a lot of money and say it's mine, without question. I know you work hard, harder than I know. I love hating how difficult you can be—because really, you can be.

I love the way we go to IKEA early on Sunday and drop our daughter at the childcare play area for up to one glorious hour. I love pushing the cart together, hands touching. I love lying side by side on the model beds, playing footsie while shoppers stroll by. I love how we stop in front of the men's room and flirt, imagining for a minute we had the courage to actually do what we're both thinking about. I can tell you're thinking about it too because you stand, agitated, for an extra couple seconds behind a low bookshelf before we move on. I love that.

I dream of how we will be. I dream our children are almost grown; they are beautiful, strong, unruly teenagers. I dream we lie to them, ditching out on soccer games and SAT preparations and their latest young dramas. We tell them we're on separate business trips, but instead we plan a rendezvous at the Starlight Motel in Reno. On

the plane I am giddy and foolish; I'm much too old for this. You're three rows up. I brush against you on the way to the bathroom and for the first time in many years, I blush.

At the motel, we pretend not to know each other, but it's obvious we do. The hotel clerk is onto us. She's seen this kind of thing before. In my dream we check in to different rooms and I flip on the TV and listen to the sounds of low-budget sex. In my dream I forget your snoring, forget how hard it has been, forget that I get bored. In my dream I sit naked in front of the mirror. I imagine you undressing me, seeing the body you have known forever. I touch myself, touch the fine white lines of various scars that map our life together: that damn motorcycle, the caesareans, places you grab me.

Tonight, in my dreams, I imagine I put on a red wig with short bangs that makes me look—I hope—young and cheap. I walk to your door wearing more makeup than usual and fewer clothes. You are surprised, but not. We drink whiskey from a bottle, and kiss, igniting lost tastes and desires and dreams. I dream you tremble at how well we fit, still, after all this time. We are a puzzle, you and I, with matching pieces, image unfinished. I dream we take pictures and giggle at the thought of our kids one day finding them.

I dream that on the plane home we hold hands and talk about buying an RV. We will travel the country solving crimes and visiting our kids who have left for greener pastures. We will hook up with other golden-agers, we will embarrass our children, we will pull the whole rig over just for a hand job. And up on the dash, along with recent photos and letters, will be a small faded mirror that will remind us of better times and worse times, and most importantly of times when it was Just Us, Always.

How to Bring out the Naughty in Your Favorite Mommy

FOREPLAY

···· **Get frisky:** Encourage her to go for a walk with you; offer to hang with the kids while she goes to the gym. Exercise increases blood flow to *all areas* of the body, if you know what I mean.

···· **Talk dirty to her:** And use your body to show you mean it. Vacuum, sweep, clean the toilet. Who cares if it's not usually your job, or if you have no idea what you're doing? She'll appreciate the effort.

···· **Get her laid:** Sleep deprivation has been used as torture; it's definitely *not* sexy. Take the kids out first thing in the morning so she can sleep in. Take on an extra midnight diaper change; it might not be your turn, but it is a turn-on.

···· **Cop a feel:** There's nothing hotter than a man close to tears; share a feeling now and then! It doesn't make you a sap; it makes you sexy.

BUILD UP

···· **Make a booty call:** Pick up the phone and arrange reliable, safe childcare your partner will approve of; don't assume she'll take care of it. If you're staying in for the night, check and change all booties. Put said booties to bed.

···· **Get fresh:** I never got over my heightened sense of smell from pregnancy. I can smell salami on my husband's breath from a mile away, and it's never a turn-on. So if she turns away from your kisses, don't necessarily take it personally. And never underestimate the desexualizing smell of baby butt or bad breath. So primp away, and pimp away.

···· **Stroke, don't poke:** I'm talking ego here, though this is good advice in lots of areas, including pool. Tell her she looks hot, you like her lips, her legs, whatever. Don't poke at her insecurities or make fun; that's so fifth grade. And whatever you do, don't joke about never having sex. Or you won't ever have sex.

CLIMAX

• • • • **Go under cover:** Literally. Don't even come in the room without a condom on, or without some other birth control method out and ready to go. There's nothing like the thought of getting pregnant again to get in the way of getting off.

• • • • **Lubricate:** Wine is good for lubricating the senses, as well as brain cells dried out by baby talk and Barney. Probe, Liquid Silk, or your other favorite water-based blend is good for lubricating vaginas made dry by nursing hormones and postpartum trauma. Keep both flowing and plentiful on the big night.

• • • • **Give oral pleasure:** Talk to her. Tell her what you thought the first time you saw her. Tell her what you think the best sex you ever had (with her, only!) was. Tell her what you want to do to her tonight.

• • • • **Release:** Let go and let it out. Laugh. Let go of those great sexpectations, and see where the night really takes you. Let out your desires, your passion, your hopes and dreams. Don't hold back, don't be shy, don't judge.

Dear Fellas,

I wanted to share with you a little about what it's like to be a co-hunter for a lost libido and tell you my three-pronged strategy for domestic bliss and hot sex. For me it breaks down to the three Cs:

1) Chat

2) Chill

3) Chores

Here goes.

CHAT

Talk about sex, write notes, draw a picture, sing a song, whatever. Not only will you get a chance to learn a bit about your partner, but the ladies go crazy for it. But the communication needs to be relaxed, too. Take it from me, bitching about not having sex does *not* lead to sex. If I knew then what I know now . . . all the late-night, blue-balled "discussions" could have been avoided if I had just said, in as nonwhiny a voice as I could:

"I'm sorry, Babe, I was just really excited to screw. And now it's hard for me to lie next to you. I'm going to grab some string cheese, watch Sports Center, and cool down. You're welcome to join me, but if you don't, I want you to know I'm not angry or trying to punish you by leaving the room. I just have a very bad headache—in my penis."

But the best part of sexual communication is that you can do it when you're not even naked. "At what length is my stubble best/worst regarding oral pleasure?" "Should I gargle with lemon water before kissing?" "Honey, I like it when you put your hands on me, but a bit of saliva now and then helps reduce chaffing."

An idle chat about whether a short stepstool in the shower would help parts line up could suddenly lead to the kid getting a playdate at the neighbors' and you getting a midday scrub.

CHILL

It's one of life's ironies that something like sex, which has the ability to get us all wound up, also requires us to relax—at least once you're out of your twenties. A buddy of mine was griping about how he and his new wife have barely had sex since the baby was born. He told me they used to have sex X times a week, but now they're barely swinging Y times a month! All I could think to say was, "Dude, stop counting, it's a recipe for frustration. I know what you're going through, and it's gonna take some time to adjust, but one day you're gonna realize what it took me four years to figure out. It's *quality,* not quantity."

If you must play the numbers game, try this equation: Rank the quality of your average roll in the hay as X out of ten. Then think about if that's as high as you want it, and how often you get that high. If you're like me, you'll find that a ten once a week beats the hell out of two fives.

CHORES

Do your chores—or don't, but you'll get a lot less action that way. This simple fact used to bother me. How could our unbridled lust for each other be derailed by something as mundane as a lack of clean sippy cups? I treated housework a lot like exercise.

I knew I should do it, I eventually did do it and felt better for it, but I didn't see what it had to do with sex. It took reading this book to finally get it through my thick skull.

The thing is, I'm a slob. I was a slob growing up, a slob in college. I was a slob when I lived alone and a slob with my roommates—male and female alike. So the idea that I might be seen as a misogynist prick just for leaving my dirty socks on the couch just didn't occur to me. Needless to say, it has occurred to my wife. So do yourself a sexual favor, fellas—share the housework. Talk to your mate about how clean a house you're shooting for and take charge. *Then* you can watch the boxing match guilt-free, secure in the knowledge that the next time either one of you wants to get busy, you haven't already killed the mood.

⁘

So there you go, fellas. The naughty mommy's man's Three-Cs plan for harmony and action. Will it work for you? Who knows. I'm still not even sure if it'll work for me on any given day, but something is working. I'm a long-married dad and I don't stress about sex. In fact, it's hotter than ever.

—JB

Acknowledgments

i would like to say thank you to:

JB, for being such a good sport, and for being my man.

my parents, for loving me, no matter what.

my daughter, Ramona, for sharing me.

my friends and family: You now know more about my sex life than you ever wanted to. And you shared more about your sex lives than I ever expected you would.

my agent, Laura Gross, for getting me to Seal.

my editor, Jill Rothenberg, at Seal; this book is yours too, you naughty thang! And copy editor Anne Mathews.

all the literary mamas at *Literary Mama*, especially Amy, Andi, Rachel Sarah, and Laura Mazer.

everyone at CSWS; we love you guys!

KEXP 90.3 FM, for musical inspiration.

Lucia Milburn, PhD, without whom things might have turned out very different for us.

Scottie and Peter, for dragging us, respectively, down to the Armadillo that fateful night.

Johnny, always, for breaking my heart and leaving me wide open.

About the Author

The Naughty Mommy, aka Heidi Raykeil, enjoys a wonderful and mostly tame life with her husband and daughter. Her writing has been featured in *Parenting* magazine and can be found in two forthcoming anthologies: *Literary Mama: Reading for the Maternally Inclined* and *Using Our Words: Moms & Dads on Raising Kids in the Modern Neighborhood.* She is an editor and columnist at literarymama.com. She lives in Seattle.

Selected Titles from Seal Press

For more than twenty-five years, Seal Press has published groundbreaking books. By women. For women. Visit our website at www.sealpress.com.

It's a Boy: Women Writers on Raising Sons edited by Andrea J. Buchanan. $14.95, 1-58005-145-6. Seal's edgy take on what it's really like to raise boys, from toddlers to teens and beyond.

Inconsolable: How I Threw My Mental Health out with the Diapers by Marrit Ingman. $14.95, 1-58005-140-5. Ingman recounts the painful and difficult moments after the birth of her child with a mix of humor and anguish that reflects the transformative process of becoming a parent.

Literary Mama: Reading for the Maternally Inclined edited by Andrea J. Buchanan and Amy Hudock. $14.95, 1-58005-158-8. From the best of literarymama.com, this collection of personal writing includes creative nonfiction, fiction, and poetry.

Es Cuba: Life and Love on an Illegal Island by Lea Aschkenas. $15.95, 1-58005-179-0. This poignant and passionate travel memoir explores an American woman's love for another country and one of its compatriots.

The Truth Behind the Mommy Wars: Who Decides What Makes a Good Mother? by Miriam Peskowitz. $15.95, 1-58005-129-4. This moving and convincing treatise explores the new-century collision between work and mothering.

The Risks of Sunbathing Topless: And Other Funny Stories from the Road edited by Kate Chynoweth. $15.95, 1-58005-141-3. These wry, amusing, and insightful stories capture the comical essence of bad travel, and the uniquely female experience on the road.